100

SPIRITUAL LEADERS

WHO SHAPED WORLD HISTORY

Samuel Willard Crompton

A Bluewood Book

This edition produced and published by Bluewood Books A Division of The Siyeh Group, Inc., P.O. Box 689 San Mateo, CA 94401

ISBN 0-912517-44-1

Printed in U.S.A.
10, 9, 8, 7, 6, 5, 4, 3, 2, 1

Editor: Tony Napoli
Indexer: Kathy Paparchontis
Designer: Kevin Harris

Key to cover illustration:
    Clockwise, starting from top left: Zoroaster, a Chinese Buddha, Mohandas Gandhi, Martin Luther, Helena Petrovna Blavatsky, Joan of Arc, Moses, and Pope John Paul II in the center.

About the Author:
Samuel Willard Crompton teaches both European and American history at Holyoke Community College in Massachusetts. He represented the College at the "Spirituality in Education" conference in Boulder, Colorado in 1997. As a teacher, he is interested in integrating secular and religious history. Crompton has written other titles in Bluewood's 100 Series, including *100 Relationships That Shaped World History* (2000), *100 Families Who Shaped World History* (1999), *100 Americans Who Shaped American History* (1999), and *100 Military Leaders Who Shaped World History* (1999).

Picture Acknowledgements: All images and photos from the Bluwood Books Archives with the following exceptions: Alaska State Museum :78; Albert Schweitzer Archives: 88; Allan Watts Educational Programs: 101; Ameen Rihani Museum: 92; Anglican Consultative Council: 106; British Museum: 59; Brown University: 94; Chinese Consulate General: 31; Church of Scientology: 99; Columbia University: 93; Director of Public Relations of Peru: 67; Edgar Cayce Foundation:: 89; German Information Center: 32, 85; Government of India Tourist Office: 14, 53; Israel Information Services: 40, 71; Italian Cultural Institute: 41; Jewish National and University Library: 74, 75, 90; Library of Congress: 62, 76, 79; Marquette University: 95; Musee Topkapi: 30; National Portrait Gallery: 29, 57; National Spiritual Assembly: 80; NYPL: 12, 33, 42, 56, 58, 61, 97; Publications Pastorales del Arzobispado: 102; St. Bonaventure University: 100; San Mateo Public Library: 11, 20, 22, 25, 27, 65, 83, 86, 107; Spanish Tourist Office: 63; Theosophical Society: 82; Time Magazine: 96; Turkish Information Office: 47; The Vatican: 91, 104: White House: 103.

TABLE OF CONTENTS

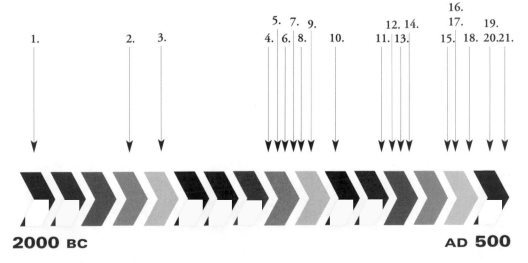

2000 BC   AD 500

TABLE OF CONTENTS

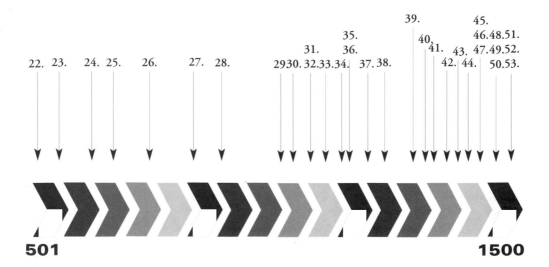

501   1500

TABLE OF CONTENTS

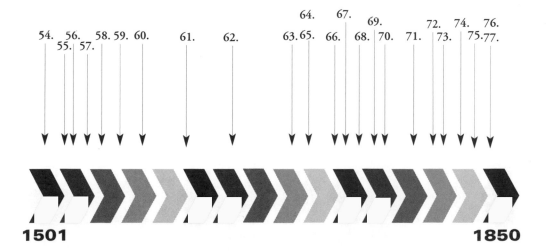

1501　　　　　　　　　　　　　　　　　　　1850

TABLE OF CONTENTS

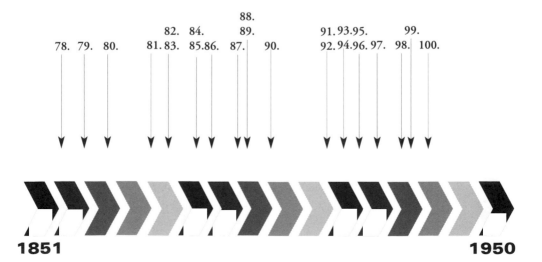

78. 79. 80.   82. 84.   85.86. 87.   88. 89.   90.   91.93.95.   99.
               81.83.   92.94.96. 97.   98. 100.

1851   **1950**

INTRODUCTION

During the late 19th century, a German philosopher claimed that "God is dead." Today, in the new millennium, many would disagree; they would respond that God is very much alive, and that people are finding new ways to God all the time.

The issue is, of course, complicated. Whose God are we talking about? Is it the Christian God, the Hebrew God (Yahweh), or the Muslim God (Allah)? And who are the true spiritual leaders? Are they the priests, rabbis, ministers, yogis, or gurus? These questions remain; no one has found any simple answers, but in searching for them, many spiritual leaders have helped to create new faiths and religious movements.

The 100 biographies in this book describe how the major—and some of the minor—faiths of the world began and have developed. Reading the entries on Moses and Abraham gives one a good idea of the tenets and foundation of Judaism. One can then go on to read about Isaac Luria and Baal Shem Tov to learn about the Kabalah and Hasidism. Similarly, a reading of the stories of Jesus of Nazareth and St. Paul tell about the formation of Christianity. However, one needs to read about St. Augustine and St. Thomas Aquinas to understand how that faith continued to develop and survive during the Middle Ages.

Sometimes, the stories tell of separation and division. The Roman Catholic and Greek Orthodox churches officially separated in 1056, and reconciliation did not occur until the mid-20th century. Until 1517, a great majority of Europeans belonged to the Catholic church. Then came the "spiritual earthquake" of the Reformation, led by Martin Luther, John Calvin, and others, and by 1550 there were Lutherans, Calvinists, Presbyterians, Anabaptists, and other Protestant sects scattered around Europe. The vessel of the One Church had been broken, and suddenly there were many competing faiths.

A fragmentation within Judaism appeared during the 18th century. European Jews found themselves divided between the followers of Hasidism, which emphasized folk remedies and faith healings, and the believers in the Haskalah, which was the Jewish Enlightenment. This breach was not healed until the 20th century.

Stories of 20th century spirituality are among the most compelling. The Dalai Lama became a sustained force for human rights in the face of Chinese totalitarianism, Pope John XXIII dramatically changed the Catholic church, and Bishop Desmond Tutu helped heal the wounds of decades of apartheid in South Africa. Meanwhile, earnest seekers such as Thomas Merton and Alan Watts traveled from West to East in search of a universal type of faith that would be common to people around the world.

The lives of the 100 men and women described in the following pages span nearly 4,000 years. In addition to the biographies of these spiritual leaders, the book also contains a glossary of more than 50 religious names and terms, some of which may already be familiar to those readers who have spent time reading about religion elsewhere. All glossary terms are in boldface, italic type the first time they appear in an entry.

Through these diverse biographies, one can find not only the beginnings of all the world's major religions and religious movements, but the numerous influential spiritual leaders who affected thousands if not millions of people looking for some spiritual guidance in their lives. And ultimately perhaps, that is the one common thread that runs through each of these stories—the desire of human beings to make some sense of their lives, to discover some purpose to human existence, and to seek answers to the eternal questions about the nature of the universe and our place in it.

1. Abraham
(c. 1800 B.C)

The city of Ur, where Abraham lived

The story of **Abraham**, the greatest of the ancient Hebrew patriarchs, comes from the first book of the Bible's **Old Testament**. It is the story of a man who learns wisdom through submission to God's will, even if it means the possible sacrifice of his own son.

Abraham was originally known as Abram. He grew up in the Sumerian city of Ur, which was located on the west bank of the Euphrates River in present-day Iraq. Eventually, Abram moved to a place called Haran, where he and his wife **Sarai** lived.

Abram was a *monotheist*—he believed in a supreme being that stood behind all the forces of nature and chance—while at this time, many people were *polytheists*. One day God spoke to Abram and told him to take his wife and his belongings and enter a land called **Canaan**, which God promised to give to Abram and all his descendants. Abram obeyed the word of God; he moved to Canaan, where he set up various altars and shrines to God.

When a famine struck Canaan, Abram and Sarai journeyed to Egypt, but later they returned to Canaan. Since they had no children, and Sarai was past childbearing years, she urged Abram to take her handmaid, Hagar, to be his concubine. Hagar soon gave birth to a son, **Ishmael**.

Soon afterward, God once more appeared to Abram and informed him that Sarai would give birth to a son. As a sign of their faith in him, God commanded Abram and Sarai to change their names to Abraham and Sarah. This was done, and within a year's time, Sarah gave birth to **Isaac**. The obedient couple rejoiced in God's favor. Yet, the presence of Ishmael, a son who was not her own, weighed on Sarah; she persuaded Abram to cast both Hagar and Ishmael out into the desert.

However, God had not finished testing Abraham. He soon was told to take his son to **Mount Moreai**, and there to make a sacrifice of the boy, showing his fealty to God. Abraham cried out in his words and in his spirit against this command, but he decided that God must be obeyed. Therefore, Abraham took Isaac to the hillside and was about to sacrifice him when an angel intervened, and ordered Abraham to sacrifice a ram instead. Abraham had passed his last and greatest test; his obedience to God was confirmed.

Abraham lived to a very old age; after his wife Sarah died, he remarried and fathered several more children, who gave him many grandchildren. After his death, the leadership of this new Hebrew clan passed to Isaac. Abraham's eldest son, Ishmael became the legendary father of the Arabs.

2. Akhenaten
(c. mid–1300s B.C.)

During the mid–1300s B.C. an Egyptian **pharaoh** boldly challenged more than 1500 years of religious traditions by worshipping only one God.

Akhenaten was the son of the pharaoh Amenhotep III, one of the most powerful and popular rulers of the 18th Egyptian dynasty. Upon the death of his father, Akhenaten ascended the throne as Amenhotep IV. He married **Nefertiti** and the couple had six daughters.

Throughout their history, the Egyptian people worshipped many Gods, one of whom was the sun-God, **Aten**. Amenhotep announced that he believed Aten was the one all-powerful God in the universe, and that all people should only worship him. Amenhotep then changed his name to Akhenaten ("One Useful to Aten"). He also moved Egypt's capital from Thebes to a city he built on the eastern bank of the Nile. He called his city Akhetaten ("Horizon of Aten"). Today the location is known as **el-Amarna**.

Akhenaten and Nefertiti presided over a court that worshipped only Aten. The names of other gods were wiped from the stone sculptures of the imperial residence, and Akhenaten required his household and courtiers to follow his beliefs. Akhenaten and his followers also created grand new buildings and held elaborate ceremonies in their new temples and palaces. The new capital gained in riches, and what has become known as the Amarna period in Egyptian art began. Sculptures became both more realistic and more lively; paintings showed the pharaoh to be oddly shaped (he had a very long neck and enormous thighs) and he and his family were depicted in informal, even playful scenes.

However, many high Egyptian priests were offended and felt threatened by the pharaoh's worship of only one God. When Akhenaten's followers began to destroy the statues and sites of other Egyptian Gods, many Egyptian people became very angry as well. By the time Akhenaten died around 1335 B.C., he had become very unpopular.

The throne soon passed to his young son-in-law, **Tutankhaten**, who was renamed Tutankhamun. Under his reign, the capital returned to Thebes; the depiction of the sun God Aten was erased from many obelisks throughout Egypt, and the people returned to polytheism, or worshipping many Gods. Eventually Akhenaten's successors destroyed nearly everything he had built in his new city, wiping away almost all evidence of his rule.

Our knowledge of this period of Egyptian history comes from excavations done at el-Amarna between 1887 and 1934. One of the greatest moments in modern archaeology came in 1922 when Tutankhamun's tomb was discovered; archaeologists and art historians thereby found the means by which to understand the legacy of Akhenaten and his family.

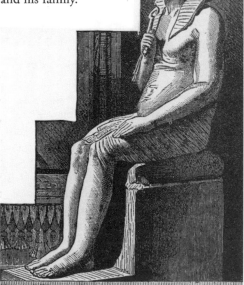

Akhenaten

3. Moses
(c. 1200 B.C.)

The story of **Moses**, who led the Hebrew people on an exodus that brought them to the promised land, comes from the Bible's **Old Testamen**t.

Sometime between 1900–1300 B.C., the Hebrew descendants of Abraham (see no. 1) had fallen into a state of bondage in Egypt; they were among the many slaves who labored to build pyramids, temples, and obelisks. Remembering God's promise to Abraham that the land of Canaan belonged to them, the Hebrews looked for a deliverer. They found him in Moses.

Moses was the son of Amram and Jochebel of the tribe of Levi, one of the 12 tribes that claimed to be descendants of Abraham. Fearful that the Hebrews were becoming too great in number, the Egyptian pharaoh had ordered that all male Hebrew babies be killed. So, when Moses was born, Jochebel put her son in an arch of bulrushes and left it on the bank of the Nile. It was found by a daughter of the pharaoh. The noblewoman adopted Moses, who was raised in pride and splendor in the palace of the pharaoh.

Eventually, Moses learned about the truth of his birth and the faith of his people. Feeling their oppression intensely, Moses killed an Egyptian overseer who abused a Hebrew slave. When the crime was discovered, Moses fled into exile.

Moses wandered into the land of Midian, somewhere in what is now the Sinai peninsula, located between Israel and Egypt. There he married a woman named **Zipporah** and they had two sons.

Moses had never forgotten the faith of his Hebrew people. In a terrifying moment on **Mount Sinai**, he saw a bush that burned but was not consumed by the flames. The burning bush told him, "I am the God of Abraham and Isaac and Jacob." This experience changed Moses into a prophet.

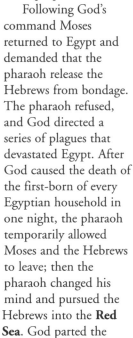

Moses with the Ten Commandments

Following God's command Moses returned to Egypt and demanded that the pharaoh release the Hebrews from bondage. The pharaoh refused, and God directed a series of plagues that devastated Egypt. After God caused the death of the first-born of every Egyptian household in one night, the pharaoh temporarily allowed Moses and the Hebrews to leave; then the pharaoh changed his mind and pursued the Hebrews into the **Red Sea**. God parted the waters to let the Hebrews cross, and then drowned the Egyptians.

Moses brought the Hebrews to Mount Sinai. The prophet ascended the mountain and spoke to God who presented Moses with two stone tablets containing a series of laws known as the **Ten Commandments**. Upon his return, Moses proclaimed that from this day forward, these were the laws by which the Hebrews must abide. These commandments have been embraced by both Judaism and Christianity, and are still the basis of morality throughout the western world.

3 1833 04095 5897

4. Zoroaster
(c. 630–553 B.C.)

Controversy remains as to the life and nationality of **Zoroaster**, but there is no doubt he was one of the most original spiritual thinkers in history. Zoroaster was a descendant of the first wave of Indo-Europeans who had moved into Persia (present-day Iran) sometime around 3500 B.C. He grew up in the small kingdom of **Avestan**, in what is now northeast Iran.

Little is known of Zoroaster's life between the ages of 15 and 30, except that he married and had several children. According to tradition, he had the first of a series of spiritual visions around the age of 30. After he spoke of these visions publicly, Zoroaster was rejected and forced into exile. Between the ages of 30 and 42, he lived the life of an itinerant preacher, one who had virtually no success in winning converts.

Perhaps this was because Zoroaster preached of a grim battle between the forces of good, led by **Ahura Mazda** (God), against the forces of evil, led by **Angra Mainyu**. According to Zoroaster, Ahura Mazda had created six Bounteous Immortals: the Good Mind, Righteousness, Devotion, Dominion, Wholeness, and Immortality. Each of these immortals was associated with one of the six good creations of God: cattle, fire, earth, metal, water, and plants. God's seventh creation was Man himself, who was intended to join the fight against the forces of Angra Mainyu, personified as Violence, Greed, and the Lie.

Zoroaster

Thus, Zoroaster preached that Man was a responsible agent who possessed free will. Man's choices were important, indeed vital, for the success of the Good in the world. This was a far cry from what most people of the day believed, which was that Man was an afterthought of the gods, an afterthought whose actions and beliefs were not very important in the universe. Those who heard Zoroaster speak must have been impressed by both the originality of his thought and the spiritual burdens they would acquire if they chose to follow his new faith.

Around the age of 40, Zoroaster made his first convert, a cousin. Two years later, Zoroaster converted **Vishtaspa**, leader of the Kavi dynasty of Avestan. Vishtaspa proceeded to convert his family and the royal court, thereby giving a legitimacy to Zoroaster's teachings. The new faith, Zorastrianism, began to spread, and it later became the official religion of the **Sassanid** dynasty, which ruled in Persia from A.D.226 until Persia was conquered by Muslim warriors. Many adherents to the faith then migrated to India, where their descendants today are known as the **Parsis**.

Little is known about the rest of Zoroaster's life. He lived until the age of 77, and may have been killed in an invasion of Persia by the Turanians.

5. Mahavira
(c.599 –527 B.C.)

The founder of the **Jainist** religion, **Mahavira** was born with the name **Vardhamana**, in the town of Kundagrama, near present-day Patna in India. He was the second son of a wealthy *Hindu* nobleman, and was raised in a state of privilege. Vardhamana entered the monastic life as a young man; he also married and had one daughter.

The birth of Mahavira

After the death of both of his parents when he was around 30, Vardhamana renounced his current life. He plucked out his hair and left the family home, determined to find a truth that was more transcendent that the family virtues under which he had been raised.

At first Vardhamana wore a simple one-piece garment. As his wanderings entered into their 13th month, he put even that aside and announced he would henceforth travel "sky-clad" (naked). Vardhamana also allowed various types of insects to infest his body, because he believed in the principle of not causing harm to any other living creature.

At around the age of 42, Vardhamana first experienced the state of **Kaivalya**, or "absolute aloneness." Believing that he had reached the pinnacle of what he could achieve through meditation and solitary endeavor, he began to teach. About this time, he began to be known as Mahavira, meaning "conqueror" (of the woes of earthly existence). His followers banded into a group and called his religion Jainism ("Religion of the Conquerors").

Mahavira accepted much of what was already believed in Indian religious practice, including **karma** and **reincarnation**. However, Mahavira went even further; he taught that karmic impurities cling to the soul in the way that barnacles cling to wood. He declared that all things—rocks, trees, plants, insects—had souls, and that it was imperative not to harm them. Finally, he taught that man's original soul had been clear and pure, but that the violent and thoughtless actions of many lifetimes had sullied it. No previous spiritual teacher had defined karma so graphically.

The answer, Mahavira said, was to cleanse the soul in this lifetime and thereby be able to quit the dreary cycle of birth, life, death, and rebirth. He preached self-reliance and urged the conquest of the four deadly sins: anger, pride, greed, and deceit. One accomplished this by practicing pacifism, nudism, and vegetarianism.

The highest achievement that a man could aspire to was to commit suicide through voluntary starvation: this was probably because of Mahavira's belief that eating caused death and pain to other life forms. He followed his own dictum; he fasted to death at the age of 72. Millions of people in India today follow the Jainist religion.

6. Lao-tzu
(c. 575–485 B.C.)

Lao-tzu was the founder of the philosophy that formed the basis of **Taoism**, one of the world's major religions.

Lao-tzu was born around 575 B.C. and lived in what is now the province of Hunan, in northeast China. We know very little about his early years, or how he rose in the Chinese government. However, by his later years, he had become curator of the royal library during the latter part of the **Chou** dynasty, which ruled China between 1027 and 256 B.C.

Lao-tzu was an older contemporary of **Confucius** (see no. 8). The younger man sought the older man out because of Lao-tzu's knowledge of mourning rituals. Confucius rose to greater prominence than the old master, however, and as his years advanced, Lao-tzu began to feel both abandoned by the society he had served, and apprehensive about the future of China. According to legend, he secretly left the capital, and rode on horseback out to the plains of western China. Foreseeing the doom of the Chou dynasty and the China he loved, Lao-tzu prepared to exit China by way of the Han-Ku Pass.

There he was stopped by a gatekeeper named Yin Hsi, who begged him not to abandon the Chinese people to their fate. Instead, Yin Hsi asked Lao-tzu to compose a book that would preserve his learning for future generations.

Impressed by the dedication of the gatekeeper, Lao-tzu took the time to write a book of 5,000 Chinese characters; it has been printed, reprinted, quoted, and revered ever since as the *Tao-te-Ching*.

Unlike Confucius's *Analects* and other classics, the Tao-te-Ching does not call for a strict code of behavior or societal reform; it speaks of naturalness and passivity as the model of a proper life. In the book, Lao-tzu describes his belief that the world order is based on the *Tao* (the way or path) that a person follows in life. On this path there is a balance between humanity and the universe, and between all the contrasting forces within both. This balance is manifested in the *ying* and *yang,* which mean the dark and sunny side of the same hill, but which symbolize the balance of opposing forces such as dark and light, male and female, weak and strong— and good and evil. In following the Tao, one applies the idea of *Te*, or virtue, which also adheres to the duality of ying and yang; it is therefore possible to have both good and bad virtue, each with its own consequence.

Lao-tzu

After completing his book, tradition says that Lao-tzu rode off into the desert. The *Tao-te-Ching* has provided spiritual enlightenment for millions of people for more than 2,500 years.

1. The Buddha (Siddhartha Gautama)
(c. 563–483 B.C.)

Siddhartha Gautama—the founder of *Buddhism*—is one of only three people to establish one of the world's major religions, the others being Jesus Christ and Muhammad.

Gautama was born in 563 B.C., the son of a local ruler on the western slope of the Himalaya Mountains in **India**. As such, he was raised in a way that would preclude him from feeling pain; the palace was full of gardens and beautiful things, and nothing in a state of decay was allowed to remain there. Thus, Siddhartha grew up in a state of virtual bliss.

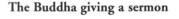
The Buddha giving a sermon

Married at age 16, Siddhartha continued to live in the palace, shielded from life's troubles. Four times he left the palace for brief intervals; on each occasion he encountered pain. He saw an old man, a sick man, a dead man, and a man committed to the religious life. These encounters with life's hardships are known to Buddhists today as the **Four Meetings**. They changed Siddhartha's life; from that point on he sought an answer to the universal problem of pain.

At the age of 29, Siddhartha chose to leave the palace. He wandered for years, observing the multitude of pains and sorrows that afflict human beings and seeking ways to alleviate those pains. He undertook studies in various other teachings, and attempted to find the answers to the questions that bothered him. However, he was unable to solve the basic problem of human life—suffering.

At around the age of 35, Siddhartha sat under a bodhi tree and began a long meditation that led him to a spirtual awakening, a full "enlightenment." He began to teach what he had learned, and soon followers flocked to him. His teachings spread swiftly and he became known as the **Buddha**, the Enlightened One.

Buddha taught the **Four Noble Truths**. First, all existence is suffering; there is no escape from the pain of human existence. Second, there is a cause for the suffering: it comes from desire. Third, release from suffereing comes from when desire ceases. Fourth, the **Eight-Fold Path** is the way to the cessation of suffering.

The Eight-Fold Path consists of: right understanding, right thoughts, right speech, right action, right livelihood, right effort, right mindfulness, and right meditation. By following this proper path (*dharma*), the soul can achieve a state of Nirvana, a perfect final state of peace.

Buddha's public ministry lasted for 45 years. He taught that **Nirvana** was open to any and all who had the courage and discipline of mind required to achieve enlightenment. Through his teachings and those of his many disciples, Buddhism arose to become one of the major world faiths.

Confucius (Kung-Fu-tzu)
(c. 551 –479 B.C.)

Perhaps the greatest of Chinese philosophers, **Kung-Fu-tzu**—later known to the world as **Confucius**—was born in the Chinese city of Ch'ufu in 551 B.C. As a young man, he tended a local nobleman's granaries and flocks, and he earned a reputation for consistency and moral uprightness. Although he rose to become a high minister in the Chinese state of Lu, Kung later lost his post as a result of the jealousy and intrigues of others. Feeling that he was a failure, he became a traveling teacher, one who imparted wisdom to young men.

Unlike some religious leaders of the time, Kung was not concerned with the afterlife; he was concerned with harmonious relations between individual persons, people within the family and within society. He believed the rules to good conduct and behavior centered upon the **Golden Rule**, *Jen*, filial piety, and the conduct of the *chun-tzu*, meaning the superior man.

The Golden Rule was summarized as "Do not do unto others what you do not wish others to do to you." The fulfillment of the Golden Rule was not simply to avoid doing harm to others, but to practice Jen, the active love of other men. Kinship and goodwill between men was crucial to this system of thought.

Kung taught that one should always respect, in fact revere, one's elders. This task did not cease upon death; it was vital for a son to make frequent visits to the graves of his parents, to bring flowers and say prayers for them. The *chun-tzu*, or superior man, was what Kung wanted to bring out in his disciples. Although he felt he had failed in government, he believed that a career in government service was the highest aspiration for any young man. Once in office, one should practice the qualities of the superior man. The *chun-tzu* was distinguished by his thoughtful-

ness and good manners and proper decorum in public. Such a man would not be easily swayed by the tides of good or ill fortune; he would work to uphold the interest of the public good. This concept of "government by virtue" led to the creation of civil service examinations in China.

Confucius

As a writer, Kung collected poems, stories, and legends and combined them into a series of books called the *Analects* that survive as classics of Chinese literature. After his death in 479 B.C., his writings continued to be widely read; eventually he was discovered by Europeans who published his works under the Latinized version of his name, Confucius. **Confucianism** is practiced today as both a philosophy and a religion by several million people, mostly in Asia.

Socrates
(c. 470 –399 B.C.)

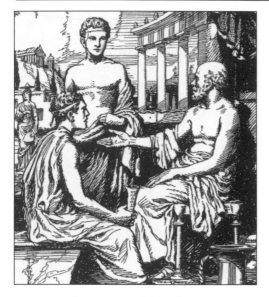

Socrates teaching Plato

The first of the great ancient Greek philosophers, **Socrates** established a system of ideas on man's relationship to the natural world that has influenced Western intellectual and spiritual thought for more than 2,000 years.

Born in **Athens**, Socrates served as a *hoplite* (heavily armed foot soldier) in three important campaigns during the **Peloponnesian War** between Athens and Sparta.

Socrates worked for a time as a sculptor before he turned to philosophy. Although he did not call himself a teacher, people flocked to him to discuss ideas. What emerged from his unofficial teaching is still known today as the "**Socratic method**," in which a teacher and his students analyze and examine an idea from all possible angles in the pursuit of truth. In the ideal situation, the Socratic teacher does not assume that his wisdom is greater than that of his students; both are engaged in a collaborative effort to arrive at the truth.

Socrates believed that humans existed for a purpose, and that right and wrong played a crucial role in defining one's relationships in the world. He also emphasized that virtue came from self-knowledge; he felt people were basically honest, and that evil was a misguided attempt to better one's own condition.

Many of Socrates' students went on to distinguish themselves in philosophy and science. Euclid, Antisthenes, Aristippus, and the great philosopher **Plato** all had their intellectual beginnings as part of Socrates' unofficial "school," which was usually conducted in the open-air market of Athens. None of Socrates' writings survive today; therefore much that we know of his thoughts comes from the writings of Plato, and the Athenian soldier, Xenophon.

Socrates' belief in a single and unified force behind the natural world contradicted the Greek belief in a pantheon of Gods. In 399 B.C., this contradiction led to Socrates' arrest and trial on charges of corrupting the youth of Athens. He refused to make a direct defense of his conduct; instead he claimed that his inner voice always guided him in the pursuit of the truth. How then could he question his own motivation?

Socrates was found guilty and sentenced to death. Plato and his other disciples visited him in prison and urged him to recant his views. Socrates replied that he had been condemned under Athenian law, which he believed to be the most just and humane system in the world. He would not recant and he would not flee the city.

Instead, Socrates chose to drink **hemlock** tea, and caused his own death. He became a source of admiration for many Athenians and his fame spread throughout the ancient world. Today he is revered for his relentless pursuit of truth and his uncompromising belief in the rule of law.

10. Zeno
(c. 335–263 B.C.)

The founder of the school of philosophy known as **Stoicism**, **Zeno**, was born at Citium on the island of Cyprus. He was probably of Phoenician descent. In 313 B.C., he was shipwrecked near the coastal town of Piraeus, which was the naval port of the city of Athens. He then settled in Athens, which was the center for Greek science and philosophy. When Cyprus was overrun by an Egyptian invasion two years later, Zeno was forced to embrace Athens as his new home.

It was a time of intellectual and cultural ferment. Numerous philosophers taught their students in the *Stoa Poikile*, a large building on the northwest part of the agora, the civic center of Athens. For about a decade, Zeno was a student of various teachers. Around the year 300 B.C., he began to teach his own philosophical tenets. He became one of the most visible philosophers there for the remainder of his life.

Athenian thought at that time centered around logic, physics, and ethics. Zeno chose to focus upon the last of these three. He taught, first, that nature is governed by an absolute set of laws that allow for no exceptions. Mankind's own nature, he taught, was that of reason. This was the only thing that separated men from animals. Zeno also declared his belief that there was no afterlife.

Zeno argued against the prevalence of passion and emotion in man's nature, declaring that these were irrational and should be rooted out of a person's makeup. Morality, he announced, was simply rational thought in action, and therefore, it was the responsibility of all men to respond to the dictates of their minds, not the whims of their feelings.

Zeno further taught that virtue was the only good, and that vice was the only evil. All virtues, he said, were equally good, and all vices were equally bad.

From this rational approach, Zeno deduced that the wise man was the good man, one who followed the path of duty. The only happiness afforded to any man was his knowledge of his own virtue, and that virtue came only from his use of rational thought and actions in support of that thought. Therefore, men should free themselves of passion, and be unmoved by either gladness or sorrow. It was especially important to submit without complaint to the demands made by life.

Zeno died at the age of 72. His philosophy continued to influence many Athenians throughout the time known as the **Hellenistic Age**, from about 300 through 100 B.C. One of his later followers was the Roman Emperor **Marcus Aurelius** (reigned A.D. 161–180) who embraced Stoicism.

Marcus Aurelius

A *pagan* once came up to Rabbi **Hillel** and offered to convert to Judaism if Hillel could explain the entire *Torah* while he, the pagan, stood on one foot. As the man raised his foot, Hillel declared, "Do not do unto others as you would not have done unto you. This is the whole of the Torah; now go and learn it." The famous and learned rabbi had made short work of his assignment.

Hillel was born in Babylonia (present-day Iraq). He went to **Jerusalem** at a young age and he earned a meager living by working with his hands. He managed to obtain some schooling, where his natural intelligence and ability came forth. Soon, he committed himself to the life of religious philosophy, and in due time he became the founder of Bet Hillel ("House of Hillel"), an academy in Jerusalem.

Before long, Hillel emerged as the leading exponent of a liberal interpretation of the Torah. He engaged in numerous debates with Rabbi **Shammai**, who led the group that argued for a conservative interpretation of Jewish law. The two men wrangled over many subjects, but it was Hillel who usually emerged victorious. This was not due to an aggressive or violent style of speech; all sources testify as to Hillel's temperance and modesty. However, during this time the mood

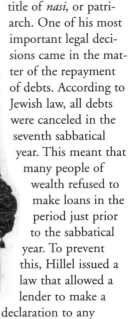

The Torah

in Jewish Palestine leaned toward liberal beliefs, and Hillel's views found favor with the majority.

Hillel became president of the *Sanhedrin*, the highest Jewish court, and he received the title of *nasi*, or patriarch. One of his most important legal decisions came in the matter of the repayment of debts. According to Jewish law, all debts were canceled in the seventh sabbatical year. This meant that many people of wealth refused to make loans in the period just prior to the sabbatical year. To prevent this, Hillel issued a law that allowed a lender to make a declaration to any court, in writing, at the time of his making a loan: "I hereby make known to you, judges of this place, that I wish to be able to collect all debts due to me at any time I may desire."

During his long period as president of the *Sanhedrin*, Hillel laid down the seven rules of *Hermeneutics*, or Bible interpretation. They were specific in listing how inferences could be drawn from principles that were quoted in two or more places in the *Scriptures*.

Hillel was so popular that the position of *nasi* was given to his family. His descendants held the title and were the official leaders of the Jewish community in Palestine for four centuries after his death.

12. Mary, Mother of Jesus Christ
(c. 22 B.C.–1st century A.D.)

All historic knowledge about the life of **Mary** is contained in the **Gospels** written by the apostles Matthew, Luke, and John, which are part of the **New Testament** of the Bible. According to Christian belief, **Jesus Christ**—the son of God born on earth in human form—was the Messiah who had come to free the people of Israel from the bonds of Roman rule and lead them to a new kingdom. As Jesus' mother, Mary occupies an important role in the theology and worship of many of the world's 1.6 billion Christians, particularly those in the Catholic church.

Historians estimate that Mary was between 16 and 18 years old at the time of her son's birth in 4 B.C. However, the precise circumstances of her death are unknown, and the Gospels provide only brief glimpses of her life. According to the Gospels, she belonged to the house of David, lived in lower Galilee, and became engaged to a carpenter named **Joseph**.

The angel Gabriel told her that though a virgin, she would conceive the son of God. She was a silent presence at her son's birth and the visits of the shepherds and Magi, and when Jesus was presented at the temple. Later, when she finds him teaching at the temple, she utters the second of three recorded statements: "My son, why have you acted so with us? Your father and I have looked for you in sorrow." Her last recorded statement was at the marriage feast at Cana when she told Jesus "They have no wine," prompting him to perform his first miracle of changing water into wine. She is last seen standing at the foot of the cross when Jesus dies.

Known from *scriptures* as the **Virgin Mary**, Christians soon began to honor Mary as the **Mother of God**—Theotokos. By the seventh century, they came to believe she had remained a virgin all her life (Ever Virgin). In the Middle Ages, Mary's perpetual purity came

to imply she was free from all sin, including original sin, later defined in Roman Catholic *dogma* as the **Immaculate Conception** (1854). In 1950, Pope Pius XII decreed that Mary, at the end of her earthly life, had been assumed into heaven, body and soul.

The Virgin Mary

Mary's reported appearances in succeeding years to fervent believers on earth has led to the building of shrines in her honor around the world. The most famous of these are the Black Madonna of Czestochowa (Poland), revered since the 14th century; the picture of Our Lady of Guadalupe commemorating an appearance in Mexico in 1531; Our Lady of Lourdes (France, 1858); and Our Lady of Fatima (Portugal, 1917).

19

The Crucifixion of Christ

A follower of one religion and the founder of another, the story of the life and times of **Jesus** was written by four of his disciples after his death, and is found in the Gospels of the **New Testament** of the Bible.

According to the Gospels, Jesus was a Jew born in Bethlehem, in Palestine, during the reign of Caesar Augustus, the first Roman emperor. Jesus grew up in Nazareth, the son of a carpenter named **Joseph** and his wife **Mary**. Orthodox Christians believe that Joseph was simply his stepfather because Jesus was literally the **Son of God**.

Around A.D. 25, Jesus became a wandering healer and teacher. A devoted and pious Jew, Jesus taught the Judaic faith into which he had grown up, but he added a new moral code that emphasized the importance of peace, honesty, simplicity, tolerance, and meekness. His most well-known message, the **Sermon on the Mount**, summarized these tenets and eventually became the essence of the foundation of a new faith.

As word of Jesus' teachings spread, so too did stories about his ability to heal the sick, cure the blind, and even, some said, to raise the dead. Before long, people were beginning to talk of him as the long-awaited **Messiah**, the savior that some Jews believed God would send to them to deliver them from their Roman oppressors, just as Moses had delivered them from Egyptian slavery around 1250 B.C.

After four years, Jesus had begun to attract many followers. He also made many enemies, in both religious and official circles, who saw this charismatic preacher as a threat to their authority. In A.D. 29 Jesus was betrayed by one of his followers, and arrested in Jerusalem by the Romans. His enemies convinced **Pontius Pilate**, the Roman governor, to have Jesus executed as a danger to Roman rule.

Jesus was nailed to a cross on a hill called Cavalry and left to die. After his burial in a tomb, according to the Gospels, he rose from the dead three days later. He appeared many times to his disciples over the next 40 days, then ascended into Heaven.

Jesus' disciples maintained that Jesus was both the Messiah and the Son of God; he was sent to earth to sacrifice his life so that all the people could be reborn in God's grace and enter into eternal paradise, or Heaven. After Jesus' death, his many followers set out to preach this message and win converts to this new religion, called **Christianity**.

Despite attempts to repress and destroy it, Christianity spread and eventually became the dominant religion of the Roman Empire. Two thousand years after its beginnings, there were 1.6 billion Christians in the world.

The most influential figure in the establishment of **Christianity**—after Jesus himself—was a Jewish tent-maker who at one time was openly hostile to the new faith and its followers.

St. Paul was born **Saul**, to a prosperous family in Tarsus, located in present-day Turkey. Saul's father was a Roman citizen, a very helpful designation which Saul inherited, and which provided a degree of security in the Roman Empire.

Saul was educated in both the **Hellenistic** (Greek) and **Jewish** traditions. While studying in Jerusalem, Saul learned of the controversy created by Jesus of Nazareth and the new sect of Christians. Seeing these people as blasphemers, Saul became a Christian-hunter, spying out Christians and dragging them before religious courts.

According to the Bible, sometime after Jesus' crucifixion, while Saul was on the road to **Damascus**, Christ appeared to him in a vision of light that blinded him. Jesus asked him, "Saul, Saul, why do you persecute me so?" When Saul asked who was speaking to him, the voice replied, "I am Jesus, the one you are persecuting! Now get up and go into the city and you will be told what to do."

Then and there Saul became a Christian convert. He went to Damascus where he was baptized; immediately, his sight returned. Soon he became passionately devoted to Christianity. He learned all he could from Jesus' disciples, and then began a plan to spread Christ's teachings to the Middle East and beyond. Over the next several years in the course of his journeys, Saul—now known as Paul, his Roman name—won converts, established churches, and wrote many letters (called epistles) describing Christian doctrine.

Unlike most early Christians, Paul believed in preaching to Jews as well as non-Jews. His success in converting members of both groups brought the anger of both Jewish and Roman authorities upon him. When he traveled to Jerusalem, he was jailed for two years.

When he was released, he journeyed to Rome; this voyage included being shipwrecked on the island of Malta, and this tale is described in the New Testament's **Gospel of St. Luke.** When he arrived in Rome, Paul met with the Apostle Peter, Jesus' hand-picked successor. Paul spent the next two years in Rome, writing and lecturing, and was recognized as a leader within the Christian community.

While the exact fate of Paul is unknown, tradition says that he was arrested and beheaded in Rome on orders of the Emperor **Nero** (A.D. 37-68), whose reign was known for its severe persecutions of Christians. Almost single-handedly, Paul had spread Christianity throughout the eastern Mediterranean. Less than 300 years later it would become the official religion of the Roman Empire itself.

St. Paul

15. Mani
(A.D. 216–c. 276)

The prophet **Mani** was born to Persian parents near Ctesiphon capital of the Parthian Empire (near present-day Iraq). The son of a father who was a member of a pious baptizing set, Mani was raised as a Christian. However, he broke away from this group because of two spiritual revelations: the first came when he was 12, the second when he was 24.

Mani spent his life in active missionary work, spreading his teachings by writing and painting. He believed strongly in the power of visual art in religious communication, and he produced a book of images to illustrate his doctrines, which came to be called **Manichaeism**.

According to these doctrines, the basic struggle in the universe is between Good and Evil, represented by the Father of Greatness and the Prince of Darkness. The soul of man has fallen into the material world, and it is trapped in an endless cycle of *reincarnation* until the Father of Greatness sends a savior to rescue those asleep in the darkness; the way to salvation is by knowledge, or direct experience of the Light.

Mani traveled to Media (western Persia), and then as far as India, but at first he found few followers. The turning point in his missionary life came when he converted Peroz, the brother of **Shapur I**, leader of the new

Shapur I

Sassanid Empire which replaced the Parthian Empire. Shapur I gave official recognition to Mani and his religion on the king's coronation day in A.D. 243.

Shapur I also gave Mani permission to preach throughout the **Persian Empire**. Many people were attracted to the new faith, and these followers were instructed to lead *ascetic* lives; they were to abstain from eating meat and from having sexual relations. The religion also preached a rejection of all violence, prayers four times a day, and a weekly confession of sins.

With Shapur's support, Mani sent his disciples to Egypt, Bactria, and Zab (near the Caspian Sea), and the faith continued to spread.

However, after Shapur's death, Mani fell from favor; the next ruler was intent on restoring Zorastrianism (see no. 4) as the empire's faith. Mani was accused of falsehood, imprisoned, and put to death.

Mani's followers were then persecuted within the Sassanid Empire; despite this persecution, the new religion persisted there up until Islamic times. In addition, Manichaeism spread west throughout much of the Roman Empire, winning new converts, the most well-known of which was the young **Augustine of Hippo** (see no. 18).

St. Helena
(c. A.D. 250–330)

While Roman Emperor **Constantine the Great** (c. A.D. 274–337) is given credit for establishing Christianity as the dominant religion of the Western world, it was the good works of his mother, **Helena**, which served to greatly spread the faith. Citing the number of churches she founded, some people have even called her the **Mother of Christianity**.

Helena was born in the ancient Roman province of Bithynia, on the coast of present-day Turkey. The daughter of an innkeeper, she met the Roman military leader **Constantius** when he passed through her district while engaged in a conquest. While it is uncertain if they married, they were together for 19 years, during which time Helena gave birth to her only son, Constantine. Around A.D. 293 Constantius abandoned Helena so he could marry the stepdaughter of his patron, Emperor Maximanius Herculius.

Constantius became emperor in A.D.305, but he died the next year; Constantine succeeded him. He then summoned Helena to his court in Rome, and conferred on her the title of Augusta, dowager empress. To further honor his mother, he renamed her birthplace **Helenopolis** and had her likeness imprinted on coins.

Some historians believe that Helena was already a Christian by this time, and that she was responsible for Constantine's conversion. Others maintain that he converted when he believed he saw a Christian symbol in the sky before he won a major battle in A.D. 312.

However, there is no uncertainty about Helena's devotion to her faith. In A.D. 324, at the age of 74, she made a pilgrimage to the Holy Land and visited **Jerusalem**. Excavating beneath the rubble of a *pagan* temple, she found pieces of wood that she claimed were remnants of the true cross on which Jesus had been crucified three centuries before. On this

Constantine

site, she founded the Church of the Holy Sepulchre. She then traveled to Bethlehem to locate Jesus' birthplace, and built the Church of the Nativity on what she believed to be that site. Although these sites have never been historically authenticated, the churches still draw thousands of *pilgrims* annually.

After founding several more churches, Helena rejoined her son, who had moved his capital from Rome to Constantinople; she died there at the age of 80. Constantine had her buried in the imperial vault of the Church of the Apostles; however, around A.D. 849, her body was transferred to the *Abbey* of **Hautvillers**, near Rheims, France. This resting place continues to be a place of pilgrimage. Helena was **canonized**, and in the Roman Catholic church her feast day is celebrated as August 18. In the Eastern Orthodox church, it is celebrated jointly with that of her son on May 21.

In the early fourth century A.D., a voice rose within Christianity to challenge the accepted view of the relationship between God, Jesus, and the Holy Spirit—and threatened to shatter the foundation of the Church itself.

Arius was born around A.D. 256, probably in Libya. He rose to become a presbyter, or priest, in Baucalis, a Christian suburb of Alexandria, one of the largest cities of the Mediterranean world.

Arius began to stir controversy when he took issue with the Church's orthodox view that God the Father and Jesus Christ were one and the same. Arius promoted his belief that God was unique and unbegotten, that everything outside of God was created from nothing by the will of God. Therefore, Arius taught, Jesus Christ was created by God the Father, and though Christ stood in a loftier place than regular humans, he was certainly not equal to God the Father.

Arius wrote and circulated verse and song to promote his view. He was censured by the Church in 318, but he continued to argue for his belief. The controversial stance—denying the true divinity of Christ—threatened to split the Church in two.

In 325, Roman Emperor **Constantine** summoned the bishops of the Church to meet at **Nicaea** (modern-day Turkey). Between 250 and 300 of them attended the conference, where they considered and debated the virtues of Arius' tenets. Arius also attended, and offered an explanation of his beliefs. However, the bishops firmly rejected **Arianism**; they condemned Arius and wrote the **Creed of Nicaea** which specifically described Jesus Christ as "begotten not made. One in Being with the Father."

However, the issue was not settled. Arius and his supporters refused to accept defeat. While the bishops labeled them heretics, Arius composed a rival pronouncement. Constantine read it and was impressed. In 331, he received Arius and ordered **Athanasius**, who had been the champion of the Creed of Nicaea, to receive Arius in communion, thereby ending the excommunication. Athanasius refused; he was deposed by the *Synod* of Tyre in 335 and exiled to Roman Gaul (present-day France). However, Arius died before he could accept reinstatement into the Church.

The debate over whether Jesus Christ was "created" or "begotten" continued until 381 when the Synod of Constantinople, with some additional changes, reaffirmed the Nicaea Creed and renamed it the **Nicene Creed**. The orthodox view had prevailed within the Roman Empire, but Arianism remained popular with large numbers of the barbarian tribesmen who lived in northern Europe. With the conversion of Clovis, King of the Franks, to orthodox Christianity in A.D. 494 the orthodox view gained steadily in strength and from then on the followers of Arianism declined.

The Nicaea Council

18. St. Augustine of Hippo
(A.D. 354–430)

The greatest theologian of the Middle Ages, and the first great philosopher-historian, **Augustine** was born in Tagaste, Numidia (present-day Algeria) in A.D. 354 His father, Patricus, was a *pagan* and his mother Monica was a Christian.

Augustine attended school at Madaurus, a center for pagan belief, and then went to Carthage (in present-day Tunisia) in 370. There he took a mistress who bore him a son, Adeodatus, in 373. During this time, Augustine became a follower of the doctrine of **Manichaeism** (see no. 15). Augustine tried to make other converts, but his energies were principally devoted to founding a school for rhetoric at Carthage.

After succeeding in Carthage, Augustine traveled to Rome and then to Milan, where he founded two other schools. He soon became dissatisfied with Manichaeism, and he came under the influence of **Ambrose**, the Christian bishop of Milan. Augustine converted to **Christianity** and was baptized on Easter Sunday in 387.

Augustine returned to Tagaste, sold the estate of his deceased father, and gave the money to the poor. He kept only a house that he turned into a monastery; it became the birthplace for the Order of the **Hermits of St. Augustine**. Augustine's son, Adeodatus, was the first to enroll in the order, but he died in 389.

News of Augustine's piety spread, and in 391 he was *ordained* a priest in **Hippo** (present-day Annaba, Algeria). He rose to become auxiliary bishop in 395 and full bishop the next year.

Hippo, Numidia, and indeed the entire Roman Empire were shocked when Gothic barbarians sacked Rome in A.D. 410. Augustine wrote *The City of God* in response to the event. In this, the master work of theology and philosophy of the early Middle Ages, Augustine contended that there were always two principal cities: the **Earthly City** (represented by Rome) and the **City of God** (represented by the Church). Though the earthly masterpieces of Rome might fall, the work of salvation, begun by Jesus Christ, and continued by all the faithful members of the Christian church, had erected a City of God so strong that nothing could prevail against it. Augustine's thesis became the background for the beliefs of millions of European Christians throughout the long period of the **Middle Ages**, (A.D. 450 –1450).

Augustine had previously recorded his own road to conversion in his *Confessions* (397-401). Together with *The City of God,* this work ensured Augustine's place as first among the learned "doctors" of the medieval church.

Augustine died of natural causes on August 28, 430, as the city of Hippo was being attacked by Vandal barbarians. The Vandals prevailed and destroyed the entire city, with the exception of Augustine's cathedral and library.

St. Augustine and his mother

19. Nestorius
(c. A.D. 381–c. 451)

A little more than 100 years after the rise of Arianism (see no. 17), another Christian heretic challenged the concept of the exact nature of the divinity of Jesus Christ.

Nestorius was born to Persian parents in the town of Germanica (present-day Syria). He went to the great city of Antioch for his education, and was *ordained* a priest in A.D. 420.

Seragio Point, Constantinople

This was a time of continuing controversy within the Christian church, which had been established as the official faith of the Roman Empire in 380. Orthodox Christians believed in the true divinity of Jesus—God and Jesus were a single being; they were opposed by those who believed that Jesus had a human nature and a divine one. The Roman Emperor thought that Nestorius might be a compromise candidate who could negotiate a middle path between Church factions, and in 428, Nestorius was appointed **Patriarch of Constantinople** (present-day Istanbul).

Nestorius's views soon caused anger and consternation among Orthodox Christians. He argued that there were two persons in Christ, instead of the orthodox view of a single person. While he did not deny Christ's divinity, he would not ascribe a divine nature to the human acts and suffering of Jesus. Nestorius also refused to call Mary the "mother of God." He argued that Jesus the Man was born to Mary, but that Jesus the Son of God could not be born to a human.

In 431, the **Council of Ephesus** considered Nestorius's teachings. The orthodox view prevailed, and on June 22, the council condemned Nestorius's doctrines and he was branded a heretic. He went into exile and spent the remaining years of his life as a wanderer in Egypt and North Africa. He died in Libya around 451.

However, Nestorius's death was by no means the end of his beliefs. Nestorius's followers lived at **Edessa** (in Syria) until 489, when they were exiled. They went to Persia and founded a theological school at Nsibis. There was already a Christian church in Persia, and the Nestorians gradually influenced it until it became known as the **Nestorian Church**, which affirmed the difference between the divine and human natures of Jesus.

The Nestorian Church flourished during the early **Middle Ages**. Nestorian monks reached China in the 8th century, and by the 13th century, the Church had spread its teachings to many places throughout **Asia**. The invasions of the Mongols, and then the armies of Tamerlane in the 14th century, effectively put an end to the Nestorians in Asia. The remnants of the Church were reconciled with the Roman Catholic church during the late Middle Ages.

26

More than 1,500 years of myth-making have obscured much of **Patrick's** life, but there is no doubt that he lived, or that he was primarily responsible for converting the Celts of Ireland to Christianity.

Patrick was born around A.D. 390, somewhere near the west coast of England. From his autobiography, we know that his father **Calphurnius** was a deacon in the Christian church; we learn nothing about his mother.

About the time he turned 16, Patrick was taken captive by marauding Irish tribes who periodically raided England's coast. He was brought to the west coast of **Ireland** and sold into slavery. After being held there for six years, he undertook a daring escape; he persuaded a ship's captain to take him aboard, and after a three-day voyage, they became wrecked on the coast of Gaul (present-day France). While it is unclear what experiences he had in Gaul, it is believed he spent several years there before finally making his way back to England.

According to his own account, Patrick had been indifferent to religion during his youth. However, he underwent a conversion during his period as a slave, and on his return to England he felt a strong need to return to Ireland and convert the people he had known there.

After studies in England and ordination, Patrick returned to Ireland. Unlike previous Christian missionaries, who had ministered to the Irish who were already Christian, Patrick made it his business to missionize throughout the Emerald Isle. Because he spoke Celtic and was very familiar with the *pagan* ways, he was able to make Christianity seem less threatening to the thousands to whom he preached.

There are numerous examples of Patrick's courageous spirit. Even if we discount the stories of how he drove serpents and snakes from the island, the historical record shows that he never swayed from his mission or his preach-

St. Patrick

ing, even though there were powerful Irish chieftains who could have had him executed.

Celtic pagan beliefs centered around the **Druid** religion, which relied heavily on magical rites and rituals performed in sacred groves of trees. To some extent, Patrick refashioned Christianity so it could accommodate many of the pagan beliefs; pagan holidays often were reconverted to Christian holy days, and the Irish converts kept their love of nature. This blend of pagan and Christian elements made up the new *Celtic Christianity*.

From the time of Patrick's death until the Viking raids of the ninth century, Celtic Christianity was probably the most vital force in Christian Europe. Most of our knowledge of early Christianity as well as the pagan legends of the Celtic world were preserved for us by Irish monks who toiled away at their manuscripts throughout the **Dark Ages** (about A.D. 475–1000).

21. St. Benedict of Nursia
(c. A.D. 480–c. 550)

The distinctive features of Western **monasticism** were introduced and developed by **Benedict of Nursia**. Never formally **ordained**, he has had one of the most lasting influences of any of the early fathers of the Christian church.

St. Benedict blessing a monk

Benedict was born to a distinguished Italian family around A.D. 480. He grew up amidst the ruin of the Roman Empire, which officially came to an end in 476, when the last emperor in Rome was deposed. It's not surprising that Benedict and other members of his generation wanted desperately to find or establish something permanent to replace the fallen empire.

Around the year 500, Benedict retired to a cave to pray and meditate, and live the life of a **hermit**. This was in the tradition of Eastern-style, individual monasticism, which flourished in Egypt, Palestine, and Syria during this time. However, Benedict's example inspired a number of other young men to join him, and eventually he found himself the

leader of a group of monks. Over the next 25 years, they founded 12 different **monasteries**, before establishing one at **Monte Cassino**, a fortified location about 1,500 feet above sea level, near Naples.

Monte Cassino was an ancient **pagan** site, with a sacred wood and two groves. Benedict destroyed the wood, and changed the groves into **oratories** dedicated to Christian saints. Then he began to compose a simple guide for his monks in their daily ritual of prayer, manual work, study, and rest. He called his guide "a little rule for beginners," and explained it was designed so as not to be too difficult for the weak, nor too easy to leave the strong unchallenged. Over time these rules would spread around the Christian world and become known as the **Monastic Rule**.

The **abbot** of the monastery was elected by his fellows, but once installed, his word was supreme within the walls. The monks owned nothing of their own; all property was held in common. They were instructed to meet in church several times a day to pray, listen to Bible readings, and meditate on them. The three key words to guide their lives were obedience, poverty, and chastity. The Rule was not strict however; monks were permitted times of relaxation.

Benedict died around 550. He was buried at Monte Cassino in the same grave as his sister, **St. Scholastica**, who had established a convent nearby. The **Benedictine** order has remained enormously important in the **Roman Catholic** church up to the present, and Benedict's Rule became the standard for all the Catholic monastic orders that followed.

22. St. Columba
(c. A.D. 521–597)

The early Middle Ages in Europe (from around A.D. 475–1000) are called the Dark Ages because so little is known about them. Rome had fallen; Latin and Greek almost disappeared, and many people believed the world was coming to an end. During this period, a small number of devoted missionaries brought the word of the Christian church to *pagan* areas. One of the most remarkable of those missionaries was **Columba**.

Columba was born at Gartan in Donegal, Ireland around A.D. 521. A member of the royal **O'Neill** family, he received an excellent basic education before he entered his monastic training at Clonard. Columba was *ordained* in 551, and within the next 12 years he founded a number of churches and several monasteries in northern Ireland.

In 563, Columba and 12 companions left Ireland for the small island of Iona, off the west coast of **Scotland**. Iona was located precisely on the boundary between Christian and pagan lands; Scotland was at that time the land of the **Picts**, who were not Christian. Iona, three-and-a-half miles long and one-and-a-half miles wide, would become the point of departure for Christian missionaries on their way to Britain (which encompassed both present-day England and Scotland).

Columba made a deep impression wherever he went. Numerous tales testify to his joyous and engaging personality. Like St. Patrick before him, Columba imbued the Christian faith with a vitality and expression that endeared him to many who would otherwise have resisted it.

Columba took a stronger step when he visited King Brude of the Picts in the Scottish Highlands in 565, thus beginning the process of converting the Picts who lived north of the Grampian Mountains. His action also eventually led to the formation of Scotland as a nation.

In 575, Columba achieved a great diplomatic feat when he mediated among the different Irish chieftains at Druim-Cetta in Ireland. By this time, Columba had given enough impetus for the creation of a Scottish Christian church, one that would be based along the lines of the Church in Ireland.

Columba died on Iona on June 9 in 597; today it is celebrated as his feast day. The monks of Iona then continued their missionary activities, establishing a central monastery at **Lindisfarne** on the eastern coast of England. It became renowned for both the strength of its missionary movement and the beauty of its illuminated manuscripts.

Lindisfarne and other areas of northern England suffered from Viking raids during the ninth century. In 849, Columba's remains were exhumed and taken from Iona to Dunkeld for protection. Columba's "Cathach," the Biblical psalms, in his own handwriting, still exists today.

St. Columba preaching to the Picts

29

23. Muhammad
(A.D. 570–632)

The man who founded the **Islamic** faith was born in A.D. 570 in the merchant town of **Mecca**, on the western side of the Arabian peninsula. He was of the Quraysh tribe, which had given up its Bedouin ways and settled in Mecca a few generations prior to his birth.

Muhammad was orphaned and raised by an uncle. At the age of 23, Muhammad entered the merchant trade and married **Khadijah**, a wealthy widow who was 15 years his senior. Muhammad wanted wealth and Khadijah wanted children. She gave birth to six children, only one of whom survived their father.

Around 610, while he was spending a period of solitude in the mountain caves near Mecca, Muhammad experienced a vision. A holy being appeared to him and said, "Muhammad, you are the Messenger of God." This being instructed Muhammad to preach a belief in one God (monotheism), and convert the people of the Arabian peninsula, who were *polytheistic*.

Other visions followed, and Muhammad began to preach in and around Mecca. (These teachings were eventually written down by his followers, and they became the **Koran**, Islam's holy *scripture*.)Later Muhammad expounded upon the five pillars of Islam: faith, prayer, the giving of alms, fasting, and the *hajj*, or pilgrimage to Mecca.

Muhammad gained some followers among the young within Mecca; however, he was strongly opposed by leading merchants, who relied heavily on idol-worship as a main source of business and income. In 620, both Muhammad's uncle and wife died. Without their support, and facing fierce opposition, in 622, Muhammad and his friend Abu Bekr fled 220 miles north to the city of **Medina**, where other tribes had expressed interest in his beliefs. Their flight became known as the "**Hegira**" and it formed the start of the Islamic calendar. In Medina, Muhammad continued to preach very successfully; he also raised an army to help spread Islamic beliefs to rival tribes.

In 630, Muhammad reentered Mecca in triumph. He smashed the 360 idols within the sanctuary, and established the rule of Allah (the "one true God") within the city. During the next two years, most of the Arabian tribes submitted to the will of the new Islamic faith.

Muhammad died suddenly in June 632. Abu Bekr then took the leadership as caliph or "successor of the Messenger of God." In the hundred years after Muhammad's death, the Islamic faith spread across North Africa to Spain, encompassed the Middle East, and spread to sections of northwest India. Today, the faith is embraced by hundreds of millions of people around the world.

Muhammad prays at the Kaaba in Mecca

Both a *pilgrim* and a scholar, this spiritual leader crossed deserts, mountains, and rivers in order to spread knowledge from India to China.

Hsüan-tsang was born in Henan province, in northeast China, the youngest of four sons of a Confucian scholar. Hsüan-tsang followed one of his older brothers to a **Buddhist** monastery, took his first vows at the age of 13, and his final vows at 20. Had he been content to work with the knowledge he had received, that would have been the end of his travels.

Instead, Hsüan-tsang found his mind burning with questions. What was India, the homeland of the Buddha, like? Was the **Pure Land** sect of Buddhism, in which he had been trained, the most spiritually rewarding, or was the new sect of **Mahayana** (Pure Consciousness) *Buddhism* even greater? The more that he posed these questions, the more convinced he became that he could not find the answers in his native country.

In 629, Hsüan-tsang exited China's western border without imperial permission. He traveled across southern Russia, and what is now Afghanistan and Pakistan in order to reach northwest India in 631. Tradition tells us that he encountered and survived tremendous hazards along the way: earthquakes, mud slides, and wild beasts.

Once in India, Hsüan-tsang went to **Magadha**, an ancient kingdom and site of the Bodhi Tree under which the Buddha had attained enlightenment. Then Hsüan-tsang

Hsüan-tsang

was invited to **Nalanda**, the greatest Buddhist monastery in India. All 10,000 of its monks and laymen turned out to greet him, and he spent two years absorbing all he could of different Buddhist teachings. He became a convert to Mahayana Buddhism, which emphasized correct consciousness over the monastic life.

In 643, after 12 years in India, Hsüan-tsang set out for China. He took only a buffalo-skin coat and a strong elephant, which carried relics, images, and the great library of several hundred Buddhist teachings he had collected.

His return trip was not nearly as hazardous as his first journey. Once he reached the Chinese border, Hsuan-tsang sent a humble message to the imperial officials, begging forgiveness for his unauthorized departure so many years ago. He was welcomed as a returning hero.

Upon the emperor's command, Hsüan-tsang wrote *Ta T'ang Hsi-yu-chi* (*The Great T'ang Record of Travels to the Western Lands*). Then he retired to a monastery and began to translate the Indian books into Chinese. He translated 76 of them before his peaceful death in 664. Over one million people attended his funeral and entombment in the Monastery of Great Beneficence. As a result of Hsüan-tsang's efforts, Buddhism continued to flourish in China long after it had begun to diminish in its birthplace of India.

25. St. Boniface
(c. A.D. 675–754)

Often called the "**Apostle of Germany**," the man most responsible for bringing Christian-ity to that land was born in Devon, England around A.D. 675.

Originally named **Wynfrith**, he was educated by the Benedictine monks at Nursling, where his scholarly aptitude became apparent. He became a skillful monk, priest, poet, and author, and could have enjoyed a comfortable life in southern England. Instead he announced his desire to missionize among the Saxon tribes of Germany.

St. Boniface preaching

Wynfrith went to Rome for the first time in 719. Pope **Gregory II** saw his eager spirit, and renamed him "**Boniface**." The pope granted Boniface wide powers to missionize in northern Europe and sent him on his way.

Boniface first went to **Thuringia**, a province in northern Germany that had been the launching point for many barbarian raids against Christian peoples in the past. Boniface impressed the Thuringians with his fearlessness; he endured taunts, threats, and was in danger a number of times. He survived these trials, and went on to missionize in Frisia (present-day Netherlands) between 719 and

721, and then in Hesse between 721 and 725. It was in the town of **Geismar**, in Hesse, that Boniface had his single greatest victory.

An oak tree dedicated and sacred to the Norwegian God **Thor** stood in Geismar. Generations of Germans had worshipped at this tree, and when Boniface approached it, people believed that a test of wills would take place between Thor and the new Christian God of whom Boniface spoke.

Rather than appear to engage in a back-and-forth struggle of wills, Boniface took his ax and cut the tree down. The Germans were horrified; surely Thor would strike down this presumptuous man. When Boniface survived, and days passed and he remained unhurt, the Germans began to declare that Boniface and the Christian God had won the victory. Boniface then pointed to an evergreen tree and named it the new holy tree, representing Christ. This is the origin of today's Christmas tree.

Boniface missionized in Thuringia and Bavaria from 725–735. By now his fame had spread, and he was able to convert large numbers of Germans and Bavarians. Boniface also built a number of religious houses for men and women throughout Germany; he believed that the division of the area into dioceses and the rule of bishops was essential for spreading the faith.

Weary of leadership, Boniface resigned all his offices in 752. He returned to the life of a simple missionary, and went back to Frisia. On June 5, 754, Boniface and 53 followers were surrounded and executed there by a group of *pagans.* Boniface's bones were brought to Fulda, the largest of the religious houses he had built.

Rabi'ah al-Adawiyya, a noted eighth century female Islamic *mystic*, was born around A.D. 730 in Basra (present-day Iraq).

A member of a very poor family, Rabi'ah had the misfortune to be seized and sold as a slave when she was a young girl. However, her master freed her a few years later when he saw her engaging in all-night prayer after a full day's work! Her remarkable piety became obvious to all who came into contact with her.

After gaining her freedom, Rabi'ah devoted the rest of her life to communing with Allah (God). She became a recluse, refusing marriage and remaining celibate. After living for a time in the desert, she returned to **Basra**, where her reputation for piety began to bring her disciples.

Rabi'ah wanted her piety to shine through everything that she thought or did. Once, when she was asked if she hated Iblis (Satan), she replied that she had room within her for only one thing: love of the divine beloved. The questioner dared to go further, and asked: did she love Muhammad? Rabi'ah professed admiration and respect for the prophet, but declared that no, she had room in her heart for only one beloved and that was Allah.

During her middle years Rabi'ah engaged in a number of intellectual and spiritual "jousts" with **Hasan** of Basra, the most renowned Islamic authority of the time. Hasan was an expert in *hadith* (oral tradition of the prophet) and he had intimate knowledge of Muhammad 's life that had been handed down to him through intellectual lineage, but Rabi'ah bested him time and again in their friendly dialogues.

Through Rabi'ah's life and witnessing, several aspects of Muslim life and belief gained greater strength. The first of these was *tawhid* (affirmation of the divine unity). Going beyond this, Rabi'ah exemplified the belief in *tawakkul*, or trust in God. This was taken to mean that a spiritual seeker should look for no rest or creature comforts in his or her journey. Third, Rabi'ah believed in *rida*, which meant a relentlessly active acceptance of the divine will. Because of this, she refused to ask God for anything other than that God should work his will in her life.

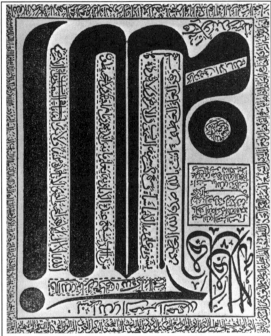

The Holy name of Allah

While Rabi'ah wrote nothing, her prayers and sayings were collected and achieved great popularity. She died in 801, and left behind a rich legacy of personal devotion and inspired mysticism. **Sufis**, who are the mystics of Islam, revere her as one of their greatest teachers. Rab'iah is the most notable among Islam's female saints, with the exception of Muhammad 's family.

27. Kukai
(A.D. 774 –835)

The Great Buddha of Kamakura, Japan

The founder of the **Shingon** sect of **Japanese Buddhism**, **Kukai** was born to a family of local nobles on Shikoku, the smallest of Japan's four islands. As a child, he was sent to a national college in Kyoto to study *Confucianism*, which had traveled from China to become the favored philosophy of the Japanese nobles. However, Kukai became disenchanted with his studies and he converted to *Buddhism*; he received ordination as a monk at the age of 19.

At first, Kukai wandered the Japanese countryside and practiced austerity in the mountains. However, in A.D. 804, he eagerly accepted the opportunity to go to China as a member of a Japanese embassy. During the two years he spent in China (804 –806), Kukai received initiation in esoteric Buddhist practices from **Huigo**, the *abbot* of the monastery of Takaosanji. When Kukai returned to Japan in 806, he brought with him sacred Buddhist texts and many ritual objects. He came back anxious to teach what he had learned.

Kukai won the favor of Emperor **Saga** (reigned 809–823), and was invited to perform ceremonies for the protection of the imperial court and the Japanese nation. In 816, Kukai received permission to build a monastery in the forests on Mount Koya. There he built **Kuyasan** ("the temple of the diamond peak"), which became the center for Shingon studies.

Shingon Buddism is based on the belief in a cosmic Buddha named **Dainichi**. The faith stresses mental and physical practices that enable adherents to realize their oneness with all living things. Kukai wrote *Ten Stages of the Mind; The Exposition of the Two Teachings, Esoteric* and *Exoteric;* and *Attaining Buddhahood in this Very Body*, all of them designed to further the spread of Shingon beliefs.

Kukai undertook many social projects as well as religious ones. He was instrumental in the building of roads, ponds, and bridges throughout Japan, as well as the construction of wells and artificial lakes. In 823, he was presented with the temple To-ji at the southern entrance to the capital city of Kyoto.

Kukai died in 835, but a legend soon sprang up that he had not died at all, that he had passed to a state of eternal meditation where he served as a savior for all suffering people until the coming of the future Buddha, known as Maitreya. Kukai—who has been known since his death as **Kobo Daishi**—remains one of the three or four great folk-heroes of Japan. Almost all Japanese villages pronounce some association they have with him; either he slept there, or he built a bridge there, or he favored the people there with his love.

28. St. Methodius (A.D. 815–885)
St. Cyril (c. A.D. 827–869)

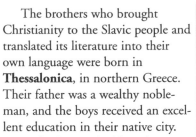

The brothers who brought Christianity to the Slavic people and translated its literature into their own language were born in **Thessalonica**, in northern Greece. Their father was a wealthy nobleman, and the boys received an excellent education in their native city.

Methodius studied law, then entered the civil service of the **Byzantine Empire**. He appeared destined for high office, but put aside his ambition to become a monk when he was around 35 years old.

Cyril studied at the imperial university in **Constantinople** (present-day Istanbul), which was the center of the Byzantine Empire. He showed great aptitude for philosophy, languages, and diplomacy. He served briefly as the librarian of the Santa Sophia (Temple of Divine Wisdom).

In A.D. 860, Cyril and Methodius went on a diplomatic mission to the **Khazars** of Caucasia. They traveled the long distance, learned the language of the people, and began to evangelize among them. On their return journey to Constantinople, Cyril discovered important holy relics, the bones of St. Clement I, in the town of Cherson on the Crimean peninsula.

Cyril began to teach philosophy at the imperial university. His life changed dramatically in 862 when Prince **Ratislav** of Greater **Moravia** (in present-day Czech Republic) asked the Byzantine Emperor to send a teacher to evangelize among his people. Prince Ratislav made a special request for a teacher who could speak to his people in their Slavonic language.

Cyril and Methodius had both spoken the language since their youth. After Michael III, the Byzantine Emperor, chose them for the mission, the brothers devised an alphabet for

St. Sophia, Constantinople

the previously unwritten Slavonic language. (It became known as the **Cyrillic alphabet.**) They then prepared a translation of the New Testament, the Biblical book of Pslams, and the letters of St. Paul into the language of the Moravian people, and performed the celebration of the *sacraments* in the vernacular.

These actions by Cyril and Methodius drew hostility from the German clergy. They believed that their own missionary efforts should have primacy over those sent by the Byzantine Emperor. There was a political issue at stake as well; Prince Ratislav wanted to gain greater independence from King Louis the German. Because of this conflict, Cyril and Methodius were summoned to Rome to report on their mission. They brought the remains of St. Clement, which won them popularity, and Pope **Adrian II** approved their use of Slavonic in the liturgy; he also *ordained* Methodius. Cyril died in Rome in 869. Methodius returned to Moravia, was appointed archbishop, and continued his work until his death.

The brothers are saints in both the **Roman Catholic** church and the **Christian Orthodox** faith.

29. Naropa
(1016 –1100)

Kashmir

Naropa is revered today as one of the 84 siddhas ("perfected ones") or **Buddhist** saints who cleansed themselves of all impurities.

He was born in northern **India** in 1016 to a **Brahman** family (the *Hindus'* highest class). Naropa went to Kashmir at the age of 11 where he undertook a three-year study of *Buddhism*. When Naropa was 16, his father required him to marry Niguma. While their marriage was satisfactory, each of them felt they had a greater calling to the religious life. They ended their union by mutual consent after eight years.

Naropa then underwent a nine-year study of Buddhism. By the time he had finished his studies, he had become renowned for his theological skill; in 1049 he became *abbot* of the fabled monastery of **Nalanda**, generally accepted to be the holiest of all the Indian places of study and worship. For eight years, Naropa stood at the very pinnacle of religious authority.

Sometime during 1057, Naropa was deeply startled by the appearance of a very old hag in his meditative visions. She told him in no uncertain terms that he was wasting his time, that true religious insight could only come through first-hand experience. Naropa asked her what he should do; her answer was that he must seek **Tilopa**, that "only Tilopa can help you."

Remarkably, Naropa followed her instructions. He resigned his position at Nalanda, officially departed from the monastic life, and set forth to find Tilopa.

Naropa wandered for 12 years. According to legend, during that time he had 11 other meditative visions, each one of which he dismissed from his consciousness, since he knew that his true task was to find Tilopa. Finally, when Naropa was on the brink of committing suicide in 1069, he met Tilopa, who informed him that the 11 previous visions had each been Tilopa himself—in disguise!

The period of trials for Naropa was just beginning. Tilopa assigned him 12 great tasks of sacrifice and surrender. Among the tasks Naropa had to undertake was to hurl himself from the top of a temple roof, to leap into a blazing fire, and to offer his body to leeches. After each of the 12 tasks his body and senses were restored to him through the grace of Tilopa. Through the agonies and ordeals, Naropa finally came to understand the necessity of surrender.

After graduating from his study with Tilopa, Naropa taught the concepts to a group of disciples. He therefore became one of the founding fathers of Tibetan Buddhism's **Kagyu lineage**, which emphasizes strict yogic discipline conducted in solitude. Today, the **Naropa Institute** in Boulder, Colorado, is one of the most important places for Buddhist study within the United States.

"I have poked into every dark recess, I have made an assault on every problem, I have plunged into every abyss. I have scrutinized the creed of every sect." These were the words of a true religious scholar, one who found that research was not enough—that personal experience was necessary for understanding.

The Muslim world experienced a decline during the tenth century. The Seljuk Turks, Central Asian horsemen, captured the city of Baghdad, and became the new rulers there. Yet at almost the same time, **Islam** found renewal in the person and career of **Abu Hamid Muhammad al-Ghazali**.

Al-Ghazali was born at Tus, near Meshed (present-day Iran). He was educated at the Nizamiya colleges of Tus, Gurgan, and Baghdad, and in 1085 he joined a group of religious scholars at the headquarters of Nizam al-Mulk, a powerful advisor of the Seljuk sultans. Continuing his rise, al-Ghazali became a professor of jurisprudence at the Nizamiya college of Baghdad in 1091.

A view of Baghdad

Like Naropa (see no. 29), al-Ghazali found his successful career to be as much of a obstacle as a benefit in his search for true enlightenment. He underwent a spiritual and intellectual crisis in 1095. He was despondent and his health failed. After resigning his position at the college, al-Ghazali left Baghdad to make his pilgrimage to **Mecca**. He wandered for the next ten years, taking up the life of a **Sufi**, or *mystic*. During this time he wrote The *Inconsistency of the Philosophers*. Had he stopped there, al-Ghazali would be remembered today only as a critic; but he went on to write *Revival of the Religious Sciences*, which is considered by many to be one of the great books of Islam. Some say it is second only to the Koran itself.

Revival of the Religious Sciences provided a discipline by which the average person could cultivate an awareness of Allah's presence in his life. Al-Ghazali believed that the true mystic experience was limited to a small percentage of people, but that by following the directions laid out in his book, others could come close to that consciousness.

Although he spent time among the Sufis, al-Ghazali did not completely believe in the mystic life. He also maintained that the language of the Sufis, which was sometimes extravagant, should not be taken literally; however close they might come to God in their higher state, a distinction between the Divine Being and the human soul still exists.

Al-Ghazali returned to his home village of Tus. He settled down to a monastic life that he shared with a group of young disciples. Before his death, he composed *The Deliverer From Error*, an autobiography notable for its charm and simplicity.

31. St. Bernard of Clairvaux
(1090–1153)

The piety, sincerity, and simplicity of a single monk inspired many Christians to help revitalize the Catholic church at the beginning of the 12th century.

Bernard was born at Fontaines, near Dijon, France into a noble family. In 1112, he entered the monastery of Citeaux, which was the mother house for the new order of **Cistercian** monks. This order believed in true monastic simplicity, whether it was in terms of clothing, or the number of hours devoted to prayer and work. Therefore, Bernard received a training that was more rigorous than that of the Benedictine monks of his day.

After Bernard was *ordained* in 1115, he and 12 companions were chosen to found a new monastery; he selected the site of

A Templar Knight

Clairvaux in Burgundy, where he would spend the rest of his days. For the next 38 years, Bernard was vigorously active on behalf of his order—transforming it from a single, modest monastery to a major order—and the Catholic church .

Through great personal charm, and a powerful presence as a preacher, this humble *abbot* became one of the most powerful figures within the church. When there was a controversy as to who should be the new pope in 1130, it was Bernard who made the decision that **Innocent II** should take the papal seat. In this, as in so many other church matters, Bernard was seen as the ultimate voice of authority: a simple monk who impressed all whom he met with his piety, strength, and sincerity.

In 1128, Bernard had been instrumental in securing church approval for the **Knights Templar of Jerusalem** as a new monastic order. This showed his belief in the crusading ideal; in 1145, Pope Eugene III, who had been one of Bernard's pupils, asked his former master to make a call for a **Second Crusade**. The First Crusade had been preached by Pope Urban II in 1095, and it was therefore a great honor for a monk to be called to repeat the performance. However, the Second Crusade never gained enough support from the kings and princes of Europe, and the attempt to dislodge the Muslims from the northern part of the Holy Land was a failure.

Largely because of Bernard's efforts, the Cisterican order brought a new vitality to the Catholic church and paved the way for the church growth that would occur in the century after his death. The great church cathedrals at **Chartres**, **Rheims** and elsewhere owe their creation to a state of religious intensity brought about by Bernard and his fellow monks.

One of the greatest female figures in the medieval Church, **Hildegard** of Bingen was many things: *mystic*, nun, writer, musician, artist, and preacher. Her life reminds us that true spiritual leaders have a way of emerging from the historical record, no matter what odds are placed against them.

During the high **Middle Ages**, women were simultaneously put on a pedestal and relegated to second-class status. Only a few women pushed beyond these boundaries. One of these few was Hildegard.

Hildegard was born near Spanheim in the **Rhineland** (present-day Germany) in 1098. She was the tenth and youngest child, and her parents gave her to the Church as a tithe offering. She grew up among the nuns of the Benedictine *abbey* of **Mount St. Disibod**. In 1136 she was unanimously elected *prioress* of the abbey. In 1150, she and 18 other nuns left their abbey and founded a new one on the Rupertsberg River near Bingen. Hildegard remained the prioress until her death.

Until she was about 40, Hildegard kept her visions secret. Since she was a child, she had seen visions of light which had directed her in her life. Once she was persuaded to commit her visions to paper, she wrote *Scivias*, which is an abbreviation for *Know the Ways of the Lord*. This book, which describes 26 specific visions, was sufficient enough to certify her importance as a mystic, but she also went on to write *The Book of Life's Merits* and *The Book of Divine Works*. In addition, she wrote a medical encyclopedia, numerous works of church music, and produced paintings to illustrate her work.

Her fame grew with each passing year. She traveled to various places in Germany to preach, including Trier and Cologne. She corresponded with bishops, kings and queens, and the pope in Rome. When she wrote to Bernard of Clairvaux (see no. 31), he authorized her visions. Many of her letters have a scolding quality; she urged the Church leaders to reform the faith, to bring it back to a more Christ-like simplicity. This was the period of cathedral-building in the high Middle Ages, and the desire for glorious buildings seemed to have outstripped the need for quiet piety. Hildegard was one of the voices that called for renewal of the values of the early Christian church.

Hildegard's last years were controversial, and for a time she was under a church ban. However, she refused to yield her strong views, and six months before she died in 1179, the ban was lifted.

Hildegard

33. Maimonides
(1135–1204)

The great Jewish religious leader and philosopher Moses ibn Maimon—commonly known as **Maimonides**—was born in Cordoba, Spain to a family of scholars. He showed his gifted intellect early, and he might have spent a comfortable life in Moorish Spain, except for the arrival of a fanatical Muslim sect known as the Almohads. His entire family left Cordoba to escape persecution, and they wandered in Morocco and Palestine before settling in **Egypt**.

After his father died, Maimonides learned medicine in order to support the family. He became a leading physician in the court of **Saladin**, Egypt's Muslim leader. At the same time, he was seen by the Jews of Egypt as their foremost rabbi, judge, and administrator.

Although Maimonides was most interested in religious philosophy, he was also deeply interested in Hellenistic science and Greek philosophy, particularly the views of **Aristotle**. Maimonides "proved" the existence of God, using formulae that had been developed by Aristotle. Maimonides also used the *mystic* strain of Judaism in his approach. He stated that it was impossible to define the inexpressible presence of God; therefore it was better to define God by what He is not. It was more appropriate to say that "God is not unjust," than to make the positive statement of "God is just." Maimonides argued that it was only possible to theorize about God's activities, not his

Maimonides

essence, which remained beyond the understanding of the human intellect.

Maimonides also wrote several other important works. His comprised the *Calendar on the Mishnah*, in which he formulated the **Thirteen Articles of Faith**. These principles affirmed traditional Jewish beliefs, were later incorporated in the **Daily Prayer Book**, and have remained the most accepted summary of the Jewish creed since that time.

In *Book of the Commandments*, Maimonides enumerated the 613 biblical commandments and put them into 14 categories. His *Mishneh Torah*, written between 1158 and 1168, was a codification of the law of the *Talmud*. Again, Maimonides devised an original structure and arrangement that made the material far more than just a restatement of previous texts. Finally, in his *Guide for the Perplexed* (1190), written in Arabic, Maimonides attempted to reconcile the science of Aristotle with the philosophy of Judaism. He argued that the Jewish faith was not an arbitrary set of doctrines, but was based on sound rational principles.

For a deeply contemplative man, Maimonides led a relentlessly active life. He remained a court physician; he wrote the greatest works of Judaic studies during his time, and he wrote ten books on medicine. It is no wonder that he was considered the greatest Jewish leader since the time of Moses.

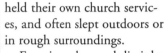

The most beloved of the Christian saints, **Francis** was born in the town of **Assisi** in Umbria, Italy. He was the oldest son of Pietro di Bernardone, a prosperous cloth merchant. During his youth, there was nothing to separate Francis from the majority of his fellows; he was high spirited, romantic, and he lived extravagantly. He was, to all who saw him, a typical impractical son of a self-made man.

Francis went on a military campaign in 1205. He was wounded, captured, and survived a serious sickness. During this time of deprivation, in the town of Spoleto he had a dream in which he heard the words, "Why do you desert the Lord for his vassal?" This awakening was spurred on by a command he heard while at prayer: "Francis, repair my house." Taking the command literally, Francis began to rebuild a crumbling church near Assisi.

Around this same time, Francis gave away his father's merchandise to feed the poor. Incensed, Pietro di Bernardone hauled his son in front of the local magistrate. Francis calmly told his father that he had no further need of him: that he would rely upon his father in heaven. As proof, Francis took off the clothes his father had given him and handed them to him.

Around 1209, Francis had another revelation; rather than rebuild churches, he was intended to spread the good news of God. From then on he traveled without food or money, relying upon the charity of the people he met. Men and women alike were overcome by his humility and simplicity; they flocked to join him.

Francis and his followers devoted themselves to preaching the gospel and caring for the poor. They also nursed the sick, (especially lepers, the most shunned of the diseased), held their own church services, and often slept outdoors or in rough surroundings.

Francis and several disciples eventually traveled to Rome where their new order received the approval of Pope **Innocent III**. The pope noted that their conduct was the closest approximation to what Christ had taught that had yet been seen.

By 1220, the **Friars Minor**, as Francis's friends were called, numbered around 5,000. In addition, a woman friend of Francis named Clare had founded a similar order for women. Then in 1221, Francis founded a "**Third Order**" for lay people who wished to dedicate their lives to helping the poor and sick while remaining in the secular world.

Late in life, Francis reportedly experienced the "stigmata," that is, wounds appeared in his hands and feet where Christ had bled on the cross. Francis died in 1226, and two years later Pope **Gregory IX** officially *canonized* him.

St Francis of Assisi

The founder of the **Soto Zen school of Buddhism**, **Dogen** was born to an aristocratic family in Kyoto, Japan in 1200. His mother died when he was two, and his father died when he was seven. Becoming an orphan so young created in him a desire to see beyond the impermanence of human life, to find something more permanent and substantial.

In 1213, Dogen took the vows of a Buddhist monk on Mount Hiei, but he experienced great doubt and soul searching. The core question with which he wrestled was: "Why is practice necessary if everyone is originally awakened to the Buddha nature?" No one within the Mahayana school of Buddhism was able to satisfy him with a response.

Many critics of Japanese Buddhism at the time claimed it had become suffocating because of its rigidity. Dogen hoped to discover a Buddhism that was more alive and penetrating, so in 1223 he journeyed to China.

The famous master **Ju-ching** (1163-1228) was the renowned *abbot* of Tiantong monastery. He tutored Dogen in the practice of *zazen*, and Dogen later reported a release from doubt and insecurity. He described this as a process of "dropping away body and mind." Ju-ching recognized the truth-seeking quality within Dogen and named him his true Dharma heir.

Dogen

Dogen returned to Japan in 1227 and wrote *A Universal Recommendation for Zazen*. The knowledge he brought won him more enemies than friends. Older Buddhist sects within Japan turned against him. However, in 1236, he established the first fully independent Zen monastery. Here he attracted many new disciples, including both men and women lay people. They followed Dogen's teachings that the essence of man and all things is the Buddha-nature, which is realized by the purification of the ego, the elimination of all selfish desires, and a complete surrender of self.

In 1243, Dogen and a small group of disciples moved to a remote part of the province of Echizen (present-day Fukui). Dogen established the monastery of **Eiheiji** ("temple of eternal peace"). He and his monks practiced a three-fold path of zazen, prayer, and study. By the time of his death in 1253, Dogen had founded the new Soto school of Zen Buddhism in Japan, based on the methods he had learned under Ju-ching in China.

Dogen's thoughts are preserved in his massive 95-volume *Shobogenzo* (*Treasury of the Right Dharma Eye*). In *Shobogenzo*, he answered the question and dilemma that had haunted him through his early years. "Sitting is the gateway of truth to total liberation." Or, as his monks would tell their initiates, "Only sit."

36. Rumi (Jalal al-Din)
(1207–1273)

Rumi was born in Balkh in what is now Afghanistan. His father was a noted **Muslim** theologian who taught in Balkh, but the family fled westward because of the Mongol invasions led by Genghis Khan. They settled in Konya in western Anatolia (present-day Turkey). Rumi spent several years in Damascus and Aleppo, perfecting his knowledge of Arabic texts. Like his father, Rumi became a teacher in Konya.

Rumi's students adored him. They behaved toward him more like a group of disciples, even though he was a philosopher and not a religious innovator. However, Rumi's life changed dramatically through the appearance of **Shams al-Din Muhammad Tabrizi**, a wandering *dervish* who came to Konya in 1244.

Rumi and Shams could hardly have been more different; the former was a trained and skilled theologian, the latter was a self-*ordained mystic*. However, the two men developed a strong bond on both a spiritual and intellectual level. According to tradition, they spent days in deep conversation, and during those times they had no need for food, exercise, or diversion—they were caught up in the spirit together. Rumi brought Shams into his house, married him to one of his wards, and began to neglect his students in favor of spending hours with the holy man.

Rumi's students drove the dervish away in 1247 and he died in mysterious circumstances that same year. However, Rumi's life had changed forever. He discarded the careful philosophy and theology he had practiced, and threw himself headlong into a search for a first-hand experience of the Divine. He became a poet, composing thousands of lyrics, many of them in Shams's name and memory.

Two other men had a profound impact on

Dervishes at prayer

Rumi. The first was **Salah al-Din Zarkub**, an illiterate goldsmith. Rumi named Salah as his spiritual successor, but Salah died first, in 1258. **Celebi Husam al-Din Hasan** lived with Rumi between 1263 and 1273. During that time, he inspired Rumi to undertake composition of the poem "spiritual couplets." The work extended to include 25,000 couplets.

Rumi died in 1273. Husam al-Din succeeded him as *shaykh* (leader) of the mystical brotherhood of **Mevlevi**. (The sect became known in the West as the "whirling dervishes" because both music and dance are central aspects of their worship). After Husam died in 1283, Rumi's son **Sultan Walad** continued the work. The brotherhood remained a hereditary order, ruled by descendants of Rumi, until 1925, when all mystical associations in Turkey were abolished by **Kemal Atatürk**, first President of the Turkish Republic.

Rumi's great contribution was to blend traditional **Arab philosophy** with **Sufi mysticism**. Because of his work and influence, the Muslim faith was renewed through the energy of mystics such as the "whirling dervishes."

Every religion has pioneers and every faith also needs synthesizers, people who bring together the beliefs into a coherent doctrine. One of the major synthesizers of Catholicism was **Thomas Aquinas**.

Thomas was born at the family castle of Aquinas in the town of Roccasecca, Italy. When he was five years old, his parents gave him as an offering to the famous Benedictine monastery at Monte Cassino. Conflicts between local nobles

St. Thomas Aquinas

led to political instability, and Thomas went home to his family during his teenage years.

Thomas joined the **Dominican Order** in 1245. Founded some 30 years earlier by Spanish-born Dominic Gunzman, the order specialized in preaching and teaching. Thomas's mother and siblings were shocked; they were all for established orders like the Benedictines, but they were suspicious of newer ones like the Dominicans. The family members held Thomas prisoner within the family castle for one year before they relented! Thomas went to Cologne and Paris to study, and then began his work as a theologian. Before long he turned to the magnificent obsession of his intellectual life: to reconcile the teachings of **St. Augustine** (see no. 18) with those of **Aristotle**.

During Thomas's lifetime, the writings of Aristotle, which had been preserved by Arab scholars, were rediscovered in the West and translated into Latin for the first time.

Thomas's life goal was to achieve a synthesis between the philosophy and theology of the Church fathers like St. Augustine and the writings of Aristotle.

For some 20 years, Thomas compiled his voluminous work. He used the writings of Aristotle, Augustine, Socrates, Plato, Plotinus, Cicero, Seneca, Arab writers, and Maimonides (see no. 33) to create his synthesis. The result was his *Summa Theologica*.

According to Aquinas, God must exist, because nature shows that there is always a first cause for everything. At the same time, he argues that one cannot believe in God simply with a scientific attitude; faith is also necessary. Having "proved" the existence of God, Aquinas went on to list specific moral virtues and personal defects that every person has to grapple with in his journey toward God.

Summa Theologica was still unfinished when Thomas had a mystical experience; on December 6, 1273, he put aside his pen and muttered that all his labors, all his writings, were "like straw beside the things that have been revealed to me." He died at a monastery in Fossanova, Italy three months later.

We get a picture of Thomas's beliefs in a quote from his *Two Precepts of Charity*, published in 1273: "Three things are necessary for the salvation of man: to know what he ought to believe; to know what he ought to desire; and to know what he ought to do."

Judaism underwent a renaissance in medieval Spain. The Islamic rulers tolerated practice of the Jewish faith, and Jews served as merchants, bankers, artists, and even diplomats. While some Jews maintained their Biblical vision of God, others tried to give God a more mystical, symbolic interpretation. One particular form of mysticism was known as the **Kabbalah**, or "inherited tradition." One of the most important of the Jewish *mystics* was **Moses de Leon**.

Moses was born in Spain. As a young man he studied the theology of **Maimonides** (see no. 33), but gradually he began to feel the pull of mysticism. Moses wandered throughout Spain, studying with various kabbalists, until eventually he settled in Avila.

Sometime around 1275, Moses wrote *The Zohar* (*The Book of Splendor*). The book is a mystical novel that depicts the third-century rabbi **Simeon bar Yohai**, wandering around Palestine talking with his disciples about God, nature and human life. The book was without structure and development of theme, and presents the idea that God resists any clear system of thought; instead, God gives each mystic a unique and personal revelation.

Moses de Leon presented the hypothesis that En Sof (God) could only become a personality, such as humans could know, through an elaborate process of ten steps. Kether (Supreme Crown or "dark flame") was the first step, followed by Hokhmah (Wisdom) and Binah (Knowledge). As God descended from Kether to Binah, God became known as "He," a masculine presence.

God, or the energy of God, then descended into Hesed (Mercy) and Din (Power, or Stern Judgment). As he proceeded down into Tifereth (Beauty), Netsakh (Lasting Endurance), Hod (Majesty), and Yesod (Foundation), God became known as "You," a being that had both masculine and feminine qualities.

Malkuth or Shekinah (Kingdom) was the tenth and final step; in this last part, God became "I," a truly personal God, such as the one that Moses encountered on Mount Sinai.

According to Moses de Leon, two things had interfered with the divine process. First, Adam had chosen to venerate the Shekinah alone, therefore pulling life and knowledge apart from one another. Second, Hesed (Mercy) and Din (Stern Judgment) had become separated from one another. Without the balancing effect of mercy, judgment had run amok, causing chaos in the world.

We know little about the rest of Moses de Leon's life. However, he had left a theory that attracted widespread attention among Jews throughout the world. His writing seemed to suggest that the deeds and prayers of men had cosmic significance, since they were needed for the divine spirit to repair and rejoin with itself. Also, the idea that God needed to (or wanted to) become personal and human showed a new importance for mankind.

The ten steps of God

45

39. Meister Eckhart
(c. 1260 –1327)

Mysticism was on the rise during the 12th and 13th centuries. Germany, which had previously been somewhat of a backwater, theologically, produced **Meister Eckhart**, perhaps the greatest **Christian** *mystic* of the Middle Ages.

Johannes Eckhart was born in Hochheim, Thuringia, Germany around the year 1260. He joined the **Dominican** friars at Erfurt, Germany, and rose to become their *prior* sometime after 1290. Around 1300, Eckhart went to Paris to study theology. There he learned from the greatest minds of his era; he remained in France for a time and lectured on Aristotelian philosophy at the University of Paris. By the time he returned to Germany, he had become a true master of mysticism.

Eckhart was one of the most dramatic and compelling speakers of his day. What we know about his theology comes to us from 59 authenticated sermons, although it is not clear whether he wrote the sermons or if they were written down afterward by some of the followers.

A Dominican monk preaching

Eckhart stressed the importance of the *Gottesgeburt in der Seele* (birth of God in the Soul). To make this possible, it is every person's job to empty himself as much as he can. Material interests and worldly desires must be cast aside in order to make the soul into a receiving station for God's being. Only when a person has done this, is the soul sufficiently attractive to bring about the *Seelenfunklein* (spark) which is part of the soul and part of God's own being, yet external to both of them.

Unlike many spiritual leaders of his day, Eckhart gave little importance to good deeds of any kind. He saw these as distractions from the main event, which was to empty and open the soul so that God could enter there. Eckhart believed that God could only be known by the mystical experience. He thought that while it was rational to believe in God, reason alone could not form any real conception of the divine nature. While the intellect could conceive of God as Three persons, only when the mystic had achieved union with God was it possible to see him as One.

In 1325, Eckhart's teachings brought him into conflict with the **Archbishop of Cologne**; in 1326, Eckhart became the first Dominican friar to be tried for heresy. He was charged with denying the goodness of God, and with claiming that God himself was born into the soul. The church later claimed that Eckhart recanted some of his heretical statements prior to his death in 1327.

Meister Eckhart was largely ignored by the Catholic church for several centuries. Then, in the late 20th century, his writings were given prominence by the Catholic theologian **Matthew Fox**, who used much of Eckhart's work in his many books.

Gregory Palamas
(c. 1296–1359)

The Christian world formally split apart in 1054, when the leaders of the Catholic church of Rome and the Orthodox church of the Byzantine Empire publicly *excommunicated* each other. The differences between the two faiths had become numerous; one of those differences was apparent in their separate approaches to the monastic life. One emphasized communal *monasticism*, and the other emphasized the importance of dwelling in the inner silence. Benedict of Nursia (see no. 21) had come to represent the life of communal monasticism; **Gregory of Palamas** became the foremost example for the **Greek Orthodox** form of monasticism.

Gregory was born in Constantinople around 1296. His father died when he was seven, and Gregory was raised as a ward of the imperial court. Imperial bureaucrats predicted a brilliant public career for the young man, but when he turned 20, Gregory and two of his brothers left Constantinople and went to **Mount Athos**, (the "Holy Mountain") in northern Greece.

Mount Athos is the most sacred spot for Orthodox monasticism. Located on a peninsula 30-miles long and 5-miles wide, Mount Athos is home to a number of monasteries. Gregory entered the monastery of the Lavra, but then left and settled at the *hermitage* of Glossia. There he received in-depth training in *hesychasm*, a method of prayer that revolved around inner silence and breathing control.

Threats of invasion by the Ottoman Turks forced Gregory to leave Mount Athos in 1325; he became a priest and lived outside the city of Thessalonki at a hermitage. He returned to Athos in 1331, and became one of the spiritual leaders of the community. As one of the leaders, Gregory was called upon to defend the monks and their hesychastic practices, when Barlaam of Cambria

denounced the brothers as men "with their souls in their navels."

Rossikon Monastery, Mt. Athos

Gregory's answer came in *Triads in Defense of the Holy Hesychasts*, published around 1338. In this book, and his subsequent lectures, Gregory asserted that hesychastic practices were the surest route to salvation. He concurred with his opponents that God's true essence is utterly unknowable, and that to assert otherwise is blasphemy. However, Gregory said, man is intended to come closer to God through participation in the uncreated energies of God. (Here he made a clear distinction between God's essence and the uncreated energies which could be entered through the silence of prayer.) Indeed, Gregory declared that man is intended to grow closer to God through prayer, and that his aim should be the *theosis* (divination) of man.

Gregory's defenses of the monastic practice won the approval of the **Byzantine Emperor** and the **Patriarch of Constantinople**. Because of his vigorous stance, the Orthodox Church remained known for its emphasis on quietude in prayer.

41. John Wycliffe
(c. 1320–1384)

During the late Middle Ages, many English people became increasingly resentful of the laws and taxes that came to them from the pope in Rome. Priests like **John Wycliffe** appeared and began to champion the idea of an English Catholic church, one that did not have to answer to Rome.

Wycliffe was born in Yorkshire around 1320. He became headmaster of Balliol College at Oxford in the 1350s; he remained closely associated with Oxford for most of his career.

John Wycliffe

Like many Englishmen, Wycliffe was perplexed and dismayed by two events that seriously divided the Church: the **Babylonian Captivity of the Papacy**, and the **Great Schism**. During the Bayblonian Captivity (1309–1377), the popes lived at Avignon in southern France, instead of Rome. They consequently favored the policies of the French kings, and sometimes appeared to be in a state of captivity that resembled the Jews in ancient Babylon.

Even worse was the Great Schism, which lasted from 1377 until 1415. During that time, there were no less than three men who claimed to be pope: one was at Avignon, another was at Rome, and the third was in Pisa, Italy. All this conflict and confusion at the highest levels of the Church led Wycliffe to develop a theological stance that led away from Roman Catholicism.

Wycliffe summarized his teachings in 33 statements that were revolutionary for their time. He stated that the Babylonian Captivity exposed the hollowness of the papacy's claims to being God's messenger on earth. Therefore, Wycliffe proceeded to explain that the true Church is made up of the "priesthood of all true believers." His basic principle was that all Christians had the right to decide religious matters by going directly to the *scriptures* and interpreting them with their own reason. This "true" Church is far more important than the "visible" Church with its hierarchy of pope, cardinals, bishops, and others.

Most controversial of all, Wycliffe attacked the doctrine of *transubstantiation*. He denied the ancient Catholic belief that the bread and wine offered at the Eucharist are transformed into the body and blood of Jesus Christ. He maintained that Christ was present only in a spiritual sense.

By 1382, many churchmen, both in England and elsewhere, were condemning Wycliffe; he had gone too far. However, Wycliffe had the support of an aristocratic patron, **John of Gaunt**, the Duke of Lancaster; in addition, by then Wycliffe's views were widely respected by many English commoners and the High Church authorities were reluctant to act against him while he was alive. Twenty-one years after his death, the **Council of Constance** condemned him as a heretic, and ordered that his bones be dug up and burned, and his ashes scattered.

42. Julian of Norwich
(1342–1416)

One of the most remarkable of the Middle Age **Christian** *mystics* was Dame **Julian of Norwich**—the details of whose life come almost exclusively from her writings of her own visionary experiences.

Julian was born in England in 1342, and we would know nothing about her were it not for her *Revelations of Divine Love*, which she wrote in two versions. We do know that Julian was an **anchoress**; she lived in a walled-up section of the Church of St. Julian in Norwich, England. This was not uncommon, as numerous mystics adopted this form of the **hermit's** life during the late Middle Ages.

From *Revelations of Divine Love*, we learn that from her youth, Julian had always desired three things: to experience the mind of Christ during his Passion, to experience a bodily sickness at the age of 30, and to receive three wounds, as gifts from God, at his discretion. Although these desires may seem extreme, variations on them were expressed by many spiritual seekers of that time.

Julian was 30 years old when she was overcome by an unnamed illness in the spring of 1373. Her friends despaired for her life, and a priest was summoned. As he waved a crucifix around her, perhaps administering the Last Rites, she experienced 15 visions over a period of about five hours. The final one came a day later, when she was out of danger.

Julian experienced a miraculous cure and her illness vanished. She soon wrote down the short version of her visions, and then spent the next 20 years in prayer and meditation before she composed her final "long" version.

As presented in the 86 chapters of Revelations, the 16 visions displayed a true window into Christian spirituality. Dame Julian saw and spoke to Christ several times. It was not a revelation of pure simplicity and goodness; Dame Julian learned that God allows good people to suffer, to endure tragedy, because he knows that their souls, their essence, are unharmed. Implied is the idea that good and evil co-exist in this world—that we cannot experience one without the other.

Julian of Norwich

Julian's writings were circulated after her death. They made a profound impact on thousands of people, who understood, through her visions, that God's plans were beneficent even though they could not be understood. Unlike many of her contemporary Europeans, Julian also perceived that God had a need for humans:

"God wills to be known and it pleaseth Him that we rest in him. For all that is beneath Him sufficeth not to us; and this is the cause why no soul is rested until all that is made be as naught to him."

43. Jan Hus
(c. 1369–1415)

By the late 14th century, followers of the English reformer John Wycliffe (see no. 41) were appearing elsewhere in Europe, leading to further condemnations from high officials in the Catholic church. One of the most noted Wycliffe supporters was the Bohemian scholar and theologian **Jan Hus**.

Jan Hus at the University of Prague

Hus was born in southwestern Bohemia (present-day Czech Republic), part of what was then the Holy Roman Empire. He attended the University of Prague between 1390 and 1396, and after graduation he stayed on to teach philosophy and theology.

In 1402, Hus became preacher at the **Bethlehem Chapel** in Prague. Founded in 1391, the chapel was the center of the Czech movement for those who wanted to reform the Church. By 1402, Hus had read the works of John Wycliffe and had become persuaded of many aspects of Wycliffe's doctrines. Hus translated many of them into the Bohemian language, and preached Wycliffe-ism from the pulpit.

In 1403, university authorities ordered him to stop proclaiming Wycliffe's views in his sermons. Pope **Alexander V** had issued a *papal bull* labeling Wycliffe a heretic, and his writings were publicly burned in Prague. However, Hus refused to comply. Twice, he was *excommunicated* from the Roman Catholic church. The second time, Hus left his beloved city so that Prague would not have to suffer and be placed under *papal interdiction*. He used this period of exile to write *De Ecclesia* (*The Church*), generally considered to be his master work.

In 1414, the different claimants to the papal throne agreed to meet at the **Council of Constance**, where Holy Roman Emperor **Sigismund** would chair the proceedings. It was vital to bring the Great Schism to an end.

Sigismund asked Hus to attend the Council. Hus agreed after the emperor gave him assurance of safety at the proceedings. As he traveled from Prague to Constance, Hus was hailed as a needed reformer by the people in nearly every town along the way. However, soon after he arrived at Constance, Hus was betrayed; he was arrested, accused of Wycliffe-ism and heresy, and imprisoned, where he remained for months.

In June 1415, the council officially condemned Wycliffe—who had been dead for 21 years—as a heretic; a few days later, it put Hus on trial. He strongly proclaimed his doctrines and refused to recant. Any neutral court would have found him innocent; instead he was found guilty and sentenced to death. He was burned at the stake on July 6, 1415.

The Council of Constance succeeded in ending the Great Schism, and by 1418 there was one pope instead of three. However, Jan Hus became one of Christianity's most famous martyrs, and his followers remained strong in the Czech lands for centuries.

The most famous female Christian martyr of the Middle Ages, **Joan of Arc** (Jeanne d'Arc) was born in Domremy, France, the daughter of an innkeeper. Joan was a devout girl; she prayed a great deal. Like most people throughout France, she was disturbed by the events of the **Hundred Years' War**, (1337–1453), which was ruining her nation. In 1420, a new treaty was signed with the English; under its terms the English held Paris and the northern half of the country, while the uncrowned Dauphin (prince Charles) of France ruled the southern half.

At about the age of 12, Joan had a vision. Three saints appeared to her; they told her she was good, to continue to pray, and that God would reveal a mission to her. The apparitions occurred several times over the next three years, and eventually the saints told Joan her task was to defeat the English, crown the Dauphin, and expel the invaders from France.

In 1429, at the age of 17, Joan went to the local fortress commander, and asked him to give her an escort of men to take her safely to the Dauphin. When Joan and her companions reached the Dauphin at Chinon on the Loire River, he was at first skeptical. However, after Joan gave him a sign of her mystical experiences, Charles gave her command of part of his army.

Joan and her soldiers liberated the city of **Orleans** in ten days. The way was now open, and she persuaded Charles to accompany her to the cathedral at Rheims, where all of the kings of France had been crowned since the time of Charlemagne.

On July 17, 1429, Charles the Dauphin became King **Charles VII** of France. Joan stood next to him, proudly holding her battle standard. She had accomplished her greatest task, and she was still only 17 years old!

In 1430, as she was leading another campaign against the British, Joan was captured by Burgundian soldiers. She was then sold to the English, who, hoping to destroy her influence, turned her over to a Church court in Rouen for trial, in January 1431.

She underwent a long and grueling interrogation; at her trial, she was accused of sorcery and heresy, for her belief that she was directly responsible to God rather than the Church. She was found guilty and sentenced to death; on May 31, 1431, she was burned at the stake. As the flames engulfed her, she was heard to cry out, "Jesus."

After the English were driven out of France, King Charles VII ordered a second trial and Joan was found innocent. In 1920, she was *canonized* by the Catholic church, and today is the patron saint of France.

Joan of Arc's vision

"Reading, reading, the whole world died—and no one became learned."

In this one sentence we can glimpse a major part of **Kabir's** teaching; that is, no holy book or holy doctrine—or even spiritual leader—can bring people to a true knowledge of God.

Kabir was born around 1440 in northeast India. Of **Muslim** birth, he was a weaver by trade; aside from that, very little is known about his early life, or how he became a wandering holy man. However, by the time he had reached his 30s, he was known throughout northern India as a poet and singer. The city of **Benares** (present-day Varanasi) is where he spent much of his time; that locality lays claim to being the center of his exploits.

Kabir was probably illiterate; certainly he never wrote his poems down. They circulated widely during his lifetime and were later published as the *Kabirvanis* (words of Kabir). As he traveled, Kabir spoke his *dohas* (popular couplets) and sang his *padas* (short songs set to refrains).

Because he spoke and sang to Muslims and **Hindus** alike, historians have sometimes said that Kabir was attempting to reconcile the two great faiths of India. Actually, he disliked both faiths, as well as all organized religions. Time and again he said that no body of doctrine, no holy book, no guru, and no yogic practice could bring one to God's grace; it could only be achieved by stripping away all externals and reaching the core of one's inner being.

Kabir rejected idolatry, traditional asceticism, and the caste system. He had the influence of a social reformer, although these traditions would outlast him. He probably made his greatest impact on the poor, illiterate Indian classes who marveled at his eloquence and set his words to their own songs. In this way, Kabir became of the greatest poets of any oral tradition in history.

One finds little comfort in Kabir's philosophy. He described life as a fleeting moment that exists between two deaths: the one that send us into the world, and the one that pulls us out. He scorned the comforts of family life, and his poetry is full of attacks on the holy men of his time. Only the inner life, according to Kabir, is worthy of a person's time and energy. If one can strip away the distractions and illusions of everyday life—including the comforts of home and family—then one may find the inner pearl of the self.

After Kabir's death, some of his followers remained Muslims; his Hindu adherents formed the sect of **Kabirpanthis**, which had more than one million members in northwest India. Kabir's disciple **Nanak** (see no. 46) became the main founder of the Sikh religion.

A view of Benares

The reformer of India and founder of the **Sikh** faith was born in the village of Talwandi, in the Punjab, in northwest India. A very bright young boy, he was not interested in playing games with children his own age. Instead, he appeared to be somewhat of a dreamer; as he got older, he seemed to lack interest in any work he attempted.

Eventually, **Nanak** married, began to raise a family, and held a respectable job as a government worker. Then one day, according to tradition, while bathing in a stream, he had a dramatic spiritual experience in which he received a calling from God. Nanak disappeared for three days in the forest, and when he returned, the first words he spoke were: "There is no *Hindu*; there is no Muslim."

Nanak believed God spoke to him, saying "thou art the divine Guru." The word *guru* means teacher. This became Nanak's great calling; from then on he was known as Guru Nanak.

In 15th century India, the country and its people were deeply divided by religion and caste, both of which Nanak would work to remove. He gave away all his possessions, left home, and became a holy wanderer. In the company of a Muslim minstrel named **Mardana**, he traveled throughout the Middle East and made his way to Mecca. One morning, Mardana was angry to find that Nanak had slept with his feet pointed west, toward the holy city of Islam. When he criticized his companion, Nanak replied, "Then show me a place where God is not."

Upon his return to India, Nanak settled in the Punjab village of **Kartarpur**, where he was soon surrounded by admirers and disciples. For the next 20 years, he espoused his ideas and devoted his time to teaching the new Sikh (meaning "disciple") faith.

Guru Nanak taught that Akal Purakh (Supreme Being) is manifest everywhere at all times. Conventional religious observances, such as attendance at mosque or temple, are less important than meditation and personal devotion. In fact, the only sure entrance to communion with God is with the spiritual guidance of a guru.

During his lifetime Guru Nanak worked tirelessly to break down the religious and societal divisions that had plagued India for some 500 years. His successors as leaders of the new

Nanak reciting poems

faith were a line of nine further gurus, the last of whom was **Gobind Singh** (1675–1708). While Nanak preached a gospel of peace, the Sikh faith unfortunately became a militant one under Gobind Singh's leadership, as the followers became warriors defending their religion against the Moguls. Today, there are more than 20 million followers of Sikhism in the world, 95 percent of them in India.

Bartolomé de Las Casas
(1474–1564)

Columbus landing in Hispaniola

A Spanish priest who traveled to the New World shortly after Columbus's voyages became one of the strongest critics of his countrymen for their treatment of the Native Americans they found there.

Bartolomé de Las Casas was born in Seville, Spain. His father was a merchant, whose modest fortunes declined throughout Las Casas's youth. In March 1493, **Christopher Columbus** returned from his first voyage to America, landing in Seville. A port city, Seville was destined to flourish because it was the entry point for the gold and silver that would eventually come from Spain's possessions in the New World. Filled with hope that they too might prosper, Las Casas's father and three uncles all sailed with Columbus on his second voyage.

In 1498, the father came home to Spain. He brought with him an Indian slave boy, temporarily given to him by Columbus. Las Casas, who played with the boy, was impressed by his vigor and manner; it was the start of a lifetime occupation of trying to save the natives from oppression and slavery.

Las Casas became a priest in 1501. He went to the Caribbean islands for the first time in 1502, and spent four years on the island of **Hispaniola** (present-day Haiti and the Dominican Republic). Las Casas made a pilgrimage to Rome in 1507, returned to Hispaniola, and then went on to Cuba. During this time he made note of the treatment of the natives, and the terrible swiftness with which they died under the twin evils of slavery and European diseases for which they had no immunity.

Las Casas made his first formal petition to help the Indians in 1515. He spent two years at the court of King **Charles I** of Spain, trying to win help for the natives. Eventually he went back to the Indies and became a **Dominican** friar. He gave up his own estates and for a time lived in the *cloister* of Santo Domingo on Hispaniola. He continued to speak out boldly against the atrocities committed against the Indians.

Las Casas's frequent petitions to Rome had a significant result. Pope **Paul III** issued a *papal bull* on June 2, 1537 declaring that since the natives showed powers of reasoning, they must be men and equals in the eyes of God. This was the first victory for the cause of just treatment of the native populations. Then in 1542, the Spanish king instituted some measure of Indian rights by abolishing slavery.

Las Casas served as bishop of Chiapas, Mexico for several years. Then he returned to Spain and penned several books. Notable among them were the *History of the Indies* and *A Brief Report on the Destruction of the Indians.*

48. Martin Luther
(1483–1546)

The man who started the ***Protestant Reformation***—and changed Christianity forever—was born in Eisleben, Germany. His father was a copper miner who wanted his son to become a lawyer. **Martin Luther** was about to begin his legal studies when on July 2, 1505, he was caught in a violent thunderstorm. Knocked to the ground, he begged St. Anne for assistance, and offered to become a monk if his life was spared. Two weeks later, he entered the order of the ***Hermits*** of Saint Augustine at Erfurt, Germany.

In 1507, Luther was ***ordained*** a priest and celebrated his first mass. In the fall of 1508, Luther was assigned to the new **University of Wittenberg** to teach ethics and philosophy. Around this time, he began to experience deep and painful doubts as to his own worthiness. After much reflection, he finally concluded that like all other men, he could do nothing to win salvation; that only his belief in Jesus and in God the Father had any merit or importance whatsoever. This eventually became known as salvation through faith.

Luther traveled to Rome in 1510, hoping to renew his sense of purpose. Instead, he was shocked by the worldly behavior and cynical attitudes of the Church leaders he met. By 1512 he returned to Wittenberg, and for the next five years he built a wide reputation as a great lecturer and preacher. He also became a fierce opponent of many of the practices of the Catholic church, especially the policy of selling ***indulgences***. The theory of a "treasury of merits," created through the good works of saints over the centuries, had been developed around 1300, and by 1517 thousands of indulgences were being sold each year.

On October 31, 1517, Luther posted his *95 Theses* (statements) on the church door at Wittenberg. Luther wanted to reform the Catholic church, not to leave it. However, Pope **Leo X** and other Church leaders refused to change their policy on indulgences. In 1521, Luther appeared before Emperor **Charles V**, the ruler of Germany and Spain. When Charles called upon him to recant his heretical beliefs, Luther refused. He was both ***excommunicated*** by the Church and forbidden the protection of lay persons by the emperor.

Kept safe by a handful of German nobles, Luther continued his work. He translated the Bible into German and also refined his doctrine, which soon became known as the **Lutheran** faith. Luther believed that the Bible is the final authority for Christians, and that salvation comes through faith alone. Having set out only to reform the Catholic church, Luther found that he had started a new faith, as well as a movement that opened the door for future reformers to create new doctrines and faiths.

Martin Luther

A Swiss priest born a year after Martin Luther (see no. 48) led a reform movement in his native country that helped the spread of *Protestantism*.

Ulrich Zwingli was the third of eight sons born to a Swiss family in the town of Wildhaus. His wealthy, devout parents urged him to become a priest, but also gave him a deep sense of the goodness, rather than the sinfulness of humankind.

Ulrich Zwingli

Zwingli was **ordained** in 1506, and that same year he settled in Glarus as the town's pastor. He led a pleasant and ordinary life there, punctuated by occasional service as a chaplain to Swiss mercenaries who served the pope.

In 1516, Zwingli was cast out by his flock, because he had turned and spoken out against the mercenary system. (In the 16th century, Swiss soldiers made up the majority of mercenaries serving throughout Europe.) After Zwingli resettled in Einsiedeln, word eventually came to him of Martin Luther and the

95 Theses. Zwingli began to believe more and more that the Roman Catholic church was corrupt, and that it needed to be reformed.

By 1519, Zwingli had become the "people's priest" at the **Great Minister Church** in Zurich. That same year, a plague swept through and claimed the lives of about one-third of the city's people. Zwingli barely survived; he emerged from the disaster more convinced than ever before of the value of faith alone and the importance of Biblical authority.

Unlike Martin Luther, Zwingli was able to use the civil authorities as allies. In 1521, he became a member of Zurich's city council, and it supported his position on the supremacy of the Bible for all civil rule. He also called for reform of the Church, with a special emphasis on ending the rule of celibacy; that same year he secretly married **Anna Reinhard**, a widow with three children.

In 1523, Zwingli presented his *67 Articles,* many of which were similar in spirit to Luther's *95 Theses.* In his articles, Zwingli opposed the venerations of saints, monastic orders, primacy of the pope, *absolution, indulgences,* and the merit of good works— all of which, as human inventions, had no basis in the Bible. With the repeated support of the city council, Zwingli had, by 1525 succeeded in creating a new "reformed" Catholic church in Zurich.

The two great reformers, Luther and Zwingli, agreed on most matters, but were thoroughly split on the Eucharist. Luther believed there was a "real presence" of Christ, while Zwingli argued that the rite was simply a memorial.

In October 1531, Catholic militia from other parts of Switzerland attacked Zurich. Zwingli died as he accompanied the troops from Zurich as a chaplain.

50. Thomas Cranmer
(1489–1556)

The man who helped King **Henry VIII** break away from the Roman Catholic church and create England's *Anglican church* ended his life as a martyr to the *Protestant* cause.

Thomas Cranmer was born in Aslacton, England, the son of a village squire. He took holy orders as a priest in 1520, just as the Reformation was getting under way in Germany. Cranmer came to the attention of King Henry VIII in 1529, when Henry was seeking some way—any way—to obtain a divorce from his wife, Catherine of Aragon, who was unable to provide him with a male heir to the throne.

Cranmer was fundamentally opposed to the long-held belief in papal supremacy. Like **John Wycliffe** (see no. 41) before him, Cranmer believed in an English Catholic church, one that should be governed by the king of England. Knowing this, King Henry appointed Cranmer **Archbishop of Canterbury** in 1533. Cranmer's first official act was to pronounce Henry's marriage to Catherine of Aragon annulled; his second was to declare the king's marriage to Anne Boleyn lawful.

During the next ten years, Cranmer and King Henry worked together to create a church that was English and Catholic, but had Protestant overtones. All financial, administrative, and judicial ties with the church in Rome were broken. In 1536, Cranmer issued his *Ten Articles*, which maintained some Catholic doctrines such as *transubstantiation*; however, it reduced the number of official *sacraments* from seven to three, recognizing only baptism, the Lord's Supper, and penance.

By 1541, the first English Bible was printed and placed in all English churches for public reading. In 1549, Cranmer produced his most important work, the *Book of Common Prayer*. Written in English, and intended for both the priests and congregations to use, the book simplified and condensed the Latin service books of the medieval church into one volume. One of the most influential religious tracts of all time, the *Book of Common Prayer* has influenced English men and women for the last 450 years.

After King Henry died, Cranmer loyally served the new, youthful King Edward VI (1537–1553), who continued the Anglican church. Edward's untimely death brought Henry's oldest daughter, Queen **Mary I**, to the throne. Mary was a devout Catholic who wanted to return the nation to Roman Catholicism; the queen quickly embarked on a program of arresting and executing leading Protestants.

Thomas Cranmer

Cranmer was imprisoned on Mary's order and knowing his danger, he made several recantations of his beliefs in writing. None of them won the Queen's mercy. He was sentenced to death, and on March 21, 1556, he publicly took back all his earlier recantations and was burned at the stake.

51. St. Ignatius of Loyola
(c. 1491–1556)

Soldier, saint, and visionary, **Ignatius of Loyola** was a remarkable leader in the **Catholic Counter-Reformation**, the 16th and 17th century revival of the church brought about by internal reform and renewed dedication to the spiritual life.

Ignatius was born at his family's castle of Loyola in Azpeitia, Spain around 1491. His parents were **Basque** nobles, and he was raised as a courtier and a gentleman. Highly attractive and charismatic, he was popular with both his men and women companions during his youth.

Ignatius entered the service of the Kingdom of Navarre in southern France in 1517. In 1521, he was badly wounded at the siege of **Pamplona**. He spent a full year recuperating, and during that time he read about the lives of Christ and the saints. Convinced that he wanted to be a soldier for Christ, rather than for any worldly kingdom, Ignatius went on a pilgrimage to **Montserrat**, Spain.

St. Ignatius

There he wrote his *Spiritual Exercises*. The book outlines a method for spiritual conversion, based on self-examination and personal decision, and emphasizes the importance of obedience to one's spiritual superiors.

Ignatius left Spain in 1522, and became a *pilgrim*. He reached Jerusalem in 1523. The Turkish rulers there did not allow him to remain, so he returned to Spain. He went to Paris in 1528, where he studied theology and attracted a group of eager disciples. In 1534, Ignatius and six followers vowed to live in poverty and chastity, and to go to Jerusalem. The group reached Venice before it became clear they could not get to the Holy City.

Consequently, Ignatius and his followers put themselves at the disposal of Pope **Paul III**, asking for difficult missions to undertake. The pope was deeply impressed by their piety, and in 1540 he approved their ventures and named them the Society of Jesus. Ignatius had created a new Catholic order; it became popularly known as the **Jesuits**. Its followers took the usual vows of poverty, chastity, and obedience, as well as vowing obedience to the pope and to undertake whatever missions he may decide are necessary.

The new order soon became highly successful. Jesuits went on missions around the known world; one of the most famous Jesuits was **St. Francis Xavier**, who missionized all the way to India and Japan.

When Ignatius died in 1556, there were more than 1,000 Jesuits serving in 12 geographic regions. By the mid-1600s, the Jesuits had established 500 schools and several seminaries and universities. Members of the order became confessors to kings, and converted many powerful nobles in central Europe. The Jesuits instituted church reform and helped stopped the spread of *Protestantism*.

58

Those who read the King James Bible today owe much to **William Tyndale**, a Greek and Hebrew scholar who dedicated his life to creating an English translation of the **New Testament**.

Tyndale was born near the border between England and Wales. While little is known about his youth, as a young man he went on to study first at Oxford, and then at Cambridge. By 1520, he had become convinced that the greatest problem with the Roman Catholic church was clerical ignorance; many priests did not know enough Latin to understand what they preached, and their congregants knew even less. Tyndale wanted to change this state of affairs.

The first English Bible

In London, he won the support and patronage of **Humphrey Monmouth**, a wealthy cloth merchant. Tyndale began to translate the New Testament from ancient Greek into English, something never done before. However, when the bishop of London showed animosity toward Tyndale and his effort, Tyndale left for Germany in 1524. He was never able to return to his own country.

Tyndale spent the next decade living in various cities, either in the Holy Roman Empire (Germany) or the Low Countries (Holland and Belgium). He started in Hamburg, moved to Wittenberg, where he met Martin Luther, moved to Cologne, and then to Worms, where his English translation was published. Copies were smuggled into England, where they caused an uproar. The bishop of London solemnly burnt copies in public, and the Archbishop of Canterbury bought many just so he could destroy them.

In 1530, Tyndale published his translation of the **Pentateuch**, the last five books of the Old Testament. He went on to write *The Parable of the Wicked Mammon*, *The Obedience of a Christian Man*, and *How Christian Rulers Ought to Govern*, which was his most important original work.

In Belgium, Tyndale was befriended by **Henry Phillips**, who pretended to agree with Tyndale's beliefs. Phillips betrayed Tyndale, and handed him over to officers of the Holy Roman Empire. He was arrested, imprisoned, and tried. In 1536, he was sentenced to death on the charge of heresy. Just before he was burned, Tyndale cried out, "Lord, open the king of England's eyes!"

Surprisingly enough, things did change in England. Prompted by his need for a divorce from Queen Catherine, King Henry VIII was in the midst of breaking away from the Roman Catholic church. Just five years after Tyndale's death, translations of the Bible were established in every English Catholic church, so that common people could read the Holy *Scripture*, which was what Tyndale had wanted all along.

53. Conrad Grebel
(c. 1498–1526)

While pioneers such as **Martin Luther** (see no. 48) and **Ulrich Zwingli** (see no. 49) helped create the *Protestant* Reformation, a group of even more radical reformers rose up to challenge Church doctrine and demand a further rejection of the tenets of Catholicism.

The rite of Baptism

Conrad Grebel was one of six children in a family that belonged to the lower level of the Swiss nobility. His father had prospered in the iron business, and Grebel grew up as a child of privilege; he studied in Basel, Vienna, and Paris, but failed to achieve scholastic merit in any of these places. By early 1522, he was back home in Zurich, where he fell under the influence of Ulrich Zwingli.

Grebel quickly converted to the new "reformed" faith in Zurich, but he became impatient with Zwingli's methods for bring-

ing about reform. While Zwingli worked carefully within the authority of the city council, and tried to bring about gradual change through procedure, Grebel wanted to cast out the entire priesthood, and establish a church that was a brotherhood of true believers. In this regard, he was following in the footsteps of both Martin Luther and Zwingli, but Grebel went one step further: he declared his opposition to infant baptism.

For hundreds of years, it had been Church policy to baptize infants as early as possible, and thereby bring them into the fold of the Church. Grebel and a small band of like-minded fellows began to assert that the Bible does not specifically call for infant baptism, and that it is much better to enter into the Church as a consenting adult, perhaps around the age of 20.

On January 21, 1525, Grebel and about 15 earnest fellow believers gathered in Zurich at the home of **Felix Mantz**, another of the radical reformers. Grebel publicly baptized George Blaurock, who proceeded to baptize others, and before the evening was over, all the congregants had been baptized.

Grebel announced that this was only a slight change from Zwingli's vision of the Church, but Zwingli and the Zurich city council disagreed vehemently. They outlawed any further such meetings; Zwingli named Grebel as the ringleader of the opposition to the reforms in Zurich.

Grebel was thrown in prison. He escaped, and left Zurich, and in May 1526 he died of the plague. Today he is known as the founder of the **Swiss Brethern**, and both the **Baptists** and **Mennonites** claim him as one of their primary spiritual leaders.

54. St. Francis Xavier
(1506–1552)

Ignatius of Loyola (see no. 51) founded the **Jesuit** order. His friend and colleague **Francis Xavier** helped spread the Jesuit word halfway across the globe.

Francis was born at the castle of Xavier in the **Basque** area of northern Spain in 1506. He went to Paris in 1525 and spent most of the next decade either studying or teaching at the university there, which was one of the great European centers of learning. In Paris, Francis found lodging with Pierre Favre and Igantius of Loyola. The three men became inseparable, and Ignatius's religious idealism began to influence Francis.

It took three years, but Igantius finally persuaded Francis to abandon his life of scholarship and devote himself to the Church. Both men were *ordained* in Venice on June 24, 1537, and the new Jesuit Order was launched.

In 1540, King John III of Portugal sent word to the Vatican that he desired help in finding people to missionize in the new Portuguese territories in **India**. Francis Xavier sailed from Portugal in 1542, beginning a ten-year odyssey that would take him to India and beyond.

Francis remained in India from 1542 until 1545. He found the people of the small European communities there cynical and indifferent to religious ways. For their part, the merchants and adventurers saw him as an enemy; several times his life was threatened, not by natives whom he was trying to convert, but by Frenchmen, Portuguese, or Spaniards.

Francis succeeded in his mission among the people of the Pearl Fishery Coast of southern India. Then, appointed *papal legate* to the Far East, he sailed from India and spent four years (1545-1549) in the **Spice Islands** (present-day Moluccan Islands of Indonesia).

On his return to India, Francis met a man named Anjiro, the first **Japanese** person he had encountered. Intrigued, Francis took a long detour and arrived in the harbor at Kagoshima in 1549. During the next two years he converted about 700 Japanese to Catholicism. Finding that the Japanese revered Chinese culture—from which they had received Zen **Buddhism** in the 13th century—Francis decided to become the first Jesuit to enter China.

He sailed from Japan, but unfortunately before he could reach China, he died on the island of Sancian, off the coast of the Japanese mainland. By the time of his death, Francis had helped convert tens of thousands of people throughout **Asia** and the **Far East**. Francis Xavier and Igantius of Loyola were both *canonized* in 1622, and Francis is the patron saint of all those involved in missionary work.

The death of St. Francis Xavier

There are leaders and there are followers—and then there are earthshakers. **John Calvin** belongs to the latter of these groups.

John Calvin was born in Noyon, Picardy, France in 1509. His middle-class parents pointed him toward the law, and he studied in Paris during the 1520s. While there, he came into contact with adherents of **Martin Luther** (see no. 48), who impressed upon him the importance of "faith and faith alone." Calvin became one of the leaders of a group of French **Protestants**, who were feared and persecuted by the French Catholic royal government.

In 1536, Calvin published a slim volume, *The Institutes of the Christian Religion.* He revised it later with many additions, but the core of his religious philosophy had already been formed by 1536, which was the year he left France for Switzerland.

John Calvin

Like Martin Luther, Calvin believed in the preaching of The Word. They felt that the Holy Bible was a greater authority than all the bishops and priests in Christendom. Calvin went one enormous step further; he declared his belief in **predestination**. A person's good works cannot save him if God has already decided that he is destined for hellfire.

Calvin arrived in **Geneva**, Switzerland and preached this gospel. The people of Geneva had already declared their freedom from the authority of the Roman Catholic church, and a movement was already underway to establish Protestantism. Although Calvin preached an extreme vision, his negative view of the possibilities open to humans seemed to strike a responsive chord with many people. Rather than use Calvin's grim theory of predestination as an excuse to reject religious ways, people seemed to strive harder to live upright, God-fearing lives. The key to this was perhaps in Calvin's continual insistence on God's omnipotence. Calvin's followers began to think that an upright life was a sign of positive predestination, and that worldly wealth might mean spiritual salvation.

A movement against Calvin arose in Geneva in 1538, and the city expelled him. However, he was called back in 1541 and given great power. He wrote a strict church ordinance, and set about making Geneva into a true **theocracy.** Church and state were united, and Calvin formulated the constitution for both. For the next 23 years, he ruled the city with an iron hand.

Calvin died in Geneva in 1564. His last request was to be buried anonymously in an unmarked grave. This was done, but his name, fame, and the word of his faith had spread. Scotland's **Presbyterian** church was formed directly from his beliefs, and the **Pilgrim** and *Puritan* fathers of New England were devoted Calvinists.

56. St. Teresa of Avila
(1515–1582)

"Let us all be mad, for the love of Him Who was called mad for our sakes." This is one of the best-known sayings of **Teresa of Avila**, one of the most prominent *mystics* of the Roman Catholic church.

Teresa de Cepeda y Ahumeda was born in Avila, Spain, one of nine children of a noble family. Her paternal grandfather had converted from Judaism to Catholicism; the family then became extreme Catholics in appearance and attitude for the sake of safety. (This was the era when those who converted were suspect and regularly persecuted in Spain.). During her youth, Teresa showed both a studious and an idealistic nature. She read stories of chivalry and romance, and she and her older brother tried to run away from home and "offer" themselves as martyrs in order to convert the Moors of North Africa. However, they were caught by her uncle a short distance beyond the town gates.

Teresa's mother died when Teresa was 15. Her father sent her to Our Lady of Grace in Avila, an Augustinian convent school; she returned home a year later because of poor health.

Teresa entered the **Carmelite Convent of the Incarnation** in Avila at the age of 20. There she enjoyed a relaxed regimen; she and her sister Carmelites had a good deal of contact with the outside world. Around the age of 40, Teresa experienced a profound conversion while she prayed in front of an image of Christ. She followed up by reading St. Augustine's *Confessions* and then experienced the first of her many religious ecstasies.

Previously, Teresa had been just one of the 140 nuns at the convent. Now she became a true spiritual leader; she set an example in prayer, and people believed that she both saw the Lord and heard him speak.

Convinced that God wanted her to lead a more active life, in 1562, Teresa founded a reformed Carmelite convent in Avila dedicated to **St. Joseph**. She took the name "Teresa of Jesus" and devoted herself to founding more convents that would emphasize a rigorous approach, rather than the moderate one she had experienced. She and her nuns were called "discalced" (meaning "without shoes"), which indicated the extent of their piety.

St. Teresa of Avila

Teresa also acted on behalf of male religious followers. She founded the first monastery of reformed Carmelite friars at Durvelo, Spain in 1568; one of the friars there was Juan de Yepes y Alvarez, who latter became known as "John of the Cross."

For 15 years, Teresa founded about one convent a year. She founded the last of them at Burgos in 1582. Teresa also wrote many books, the most notable of which was *The Interior Castle*. She was *canonized* in 1622.

57. Hiawatha
(c. 1500s)

Immortalized in Henry Wadsworth Longfellow's epic poem, "The Song of Hiawatha" (1855), the **Iroquois** leader used spiritualism to help bring peace to the Indian tribes of the future upstate region of New York.

Hiawatha was an **Onondaga** warrior who lived sometime during the mid-16th century, at the central village of his tribe where present-day Syracuse, New York is located. A fierce warrior, Hiawatha was also a cannibal who ate the bodies of his fallen foes. One day, while he was making a stew, Hiawatha saw reflected in the pot the peaceful, harmonious face of **Deganawida** standing over him. Startled and amazed, Hiawatha was soon converted by Deagnawida to the **Great Law of Peace**.

Deganawida was a Huron Indian *mystic* who had received a spiritual call to bring peace to the warring tribes in what is now New York. According to legend, he came across Lake Ontario in a white, stone canoe. That trip was the first of his miracles; the second was his conversion of Hiawatha.

At this time, tribal warfare was vicious and intense between the five tribes of the **Mohawk River Valley**—the Seneca, Cayuga, Onondaga, Oneida, and Mohawk. It was to these troubled peoples that Deganawida and Hiawatha brought their message of peace.

Because he had a speech impediment, Deganawida left the talking and persuading to Hiawatha, who became the leader for the peace mission. Both men allowed themselves to be adopted into the Mohawk tribe, and they had great success winning converts to the cause of peace.

One of their few failures came in the person of the Onondaga chieftain Atotarho. Refusing to give up his ways, Atotharo cast a spell that brought death to the wife and three children of Hiawatha. Stricken with grief, Hiawatha wandered in the woods for some time, until he discovered the use of shell or porcelain beads (today we call them wampum) for the art of condolence and requickening. By holding onto a piece or string of wampum, and reciting the Requickening Song, a person could both relive his past grievings and move beyond them.

Returning to his village, Hiawatha joined forces with Deganawida. Together, they first overcame and then persuaded Atotarho to follow the way of peace. They planted the **Great Tree of Peace** at Onondaga village, and established a balance between the five tribes of the region. Hiawatha and Deganawida convinced the Mohawk, Seneca, Oneida, Cayuga and Onondaga to band together in a confederacy that would unite their strengths, but still allow them a degree of independence. These tribes became the powerful Iroquois confederacy, who remained at peace amongst themselves, but were greatly feared by other Indian tribes, and by the white settlers who came 100 years later.

Hiawatha

During the 16th century, a renaissance took place in Jewish culture and thought. One of the places that it occurred was in Safed, **Palestine**, and one of its most remarkable new leaders was **Isaac Luria.**

Isaac ben Solomon Ashkenazi Luria was born in Jerusalem in 1534. His father had emigrated from Germany to Palestine, which was a province within the Turkish Ottoman Empire. After his father died, Isaac Luria and his mother went to Egypt where they lived with Luria's uncle, a well-to-do Cairo merchant.

Luria returned to Palestine and settled in Safed in 1569. He was surrounded by a group of disciples who venerated his every word, particularly his descriptions of heavenly visions. They called him *Ari Hakadosh* ("the Holy Lion"). Luria died at the young age of 38. He left no body of written work; our knowledge of his theology is based on conversations with his disciples, and comes from the writings of two of them—**Hayim Vital** and **Joseph ibn Tabul**.

Luria expanded on the work of the **Kabbalist *mystic* Moses de Leon** (see no. 38). De Leon had expounded on the ten spheres of activity that God had gone through in order to make himself comprehensible to mankind. De Leon had seen the critical error occur at the point where Judgment had been separated from Mercy. Luria went further, saying that God had first been required to withdraw within himself, and even away from a part of himself, in order to allow for the creation of the world and mankind. Luria also believed that the critical flaw that had prevented perfection was that when God was breathing his essence into the lower six of the spheres of activity, the "vessels" that contained God's energies had broken. Thus, God was not fully himself, and could not reveal himself to man.

Luria's philosophy acquired a great deal of meaning for Jews in the wake of their exile from Spain. In 1492, the Spanish Jews were given the harsh choice of conversion to Christianity or death. Over 150,000 had fled Spain. The expulsion was seen as the greatest disaster in Jewish history since the fall of the Temple in Jerusalem in A.D.70.

Luria's work allowed Jews to see their expulsion—indeed their state of homelessness—as part of the greater dislocation that had occurred within the very energies of God. The only remedy for the separation between the four higher and six lower spheres would come from the prayer and devotion of all men, but most especially the Jews. Luria's teaching spread to Jewish communities throughout Europe and the Middle East. It gave new hope to displaced Jews living in oppressed circumstances throughout Europe and the Mediterranean.

The expulsion of the Jews from Spain

The Dalai Lama told Altan Khan that he was the reincarnation of Kublai Khan (above)

Known as the "Rooftop of the World," **Tibet** has long been seen as a place where ancient mysteries have endured. Located north of India, south of Mongolia, and west of China, this land has produced thousands of spiritual leaders known as "*lamas*." One of the most important of these leaders is **Sonam Gyatso**, the Third **Dalai Lama**.

Gyatso was the *abbot* of a major Tibetan monastery. He was the leader of the **Yellow Hat School** of Tibetan *Buddhism*, which had been established in the 13th century. The school's main rival was the **Red Hat School** of Buddhism; the two sects quarreled over lineage, doctrine, and important questions about *reincarnation*. By the time Gyatso became abbot, the conflict between the two schools was ready to come to a head.

In 1583, Gyatso received an invitation to travel north and meet **Altan Khan**, prince of the **Mongol** tribes. The Khan, who was a descendant of the great Mongol warrior Genghis Khan, wanted to emulate his famous ancestor and reunite all the Mongolian tribes. For his part, Gyatso wanted support from the prince in his contest with the Red Hat School. So, he left Tibet and went to Mongolia to meet Khan.

The two men took a liking to one another; Gyatso told the Khan that he was a reincarnation of Kublai Khan, a grandson of Genghis and the one who had brought all of China under the rule of the Mongols. In return, the prince called Gyatso "Dalai Lama," the first known use of the term. "Dalai" was the Mongol word for ocean and "Lama" was the Tibetan word for master teacher, so bringing the two words together meant roughly: "He whose teaching is as wide as the ocean."

Gyatso gratefully accepted his new designation. He applied it to two prominent leaders of the Yellow Hat School who had come before him, **Geddun Truppa** and **Gendun Gyatso**. He named them the First and Second Dalai Lamas, with himself as the third.

There was also an important and unintended result of the meeting. In the generation after Gyatso's visit, Buddhist monks went north to Mongolia and began to establish monasteries. By the mid-1600s, most of the people living in what is now Mongolia had become Buddhist. It was a remarkable change; the Mongols had been *animists* throughout their long history.

When Gyatso died in 1588, his followers began the search for a new Dali Lama; a search, that by custom, would find a boy in whom Gyatso had been reincarnated. The boy who was found was a great-grandson of the Khan. He became the Fourth Dalai Lama and the only one of the 14 who was not an ethnic Tibetan.

Martin de Porres was one of the most active and humble saints in the history of the Catholic church.

In 1579, a son was born to Ana Velasquez, a free African woman, in Lima, **Peru**. The birth certificate declared "father unknown;" however, when the child was eight years old, Don Juan de Porres, a Spanish nobleman, acknowledged his paternity and paid for Martin's education.

At the age of 12, Martin became an apprentice to a barber/physician in Lima. The young boy showed a great gift for healing, and he worked extensively among the city's poor people. Then he asked to be admitted as a lay helper to the **Dominican** monastery of the Most Holy Rosary in Lima. At the time, he did not think himself worthy to be admitted as a full *religious*.

Because of his training with the physician, Martin was put in charge of the monastery infirmary. Serving the community of more than 300 people became Martin's task, and he performed it with skill and humility. He took seriously St. Paul's declaration in his Letters to the Corinthians that, "Charity is to be preferred before all other gifts."

Martin's fellow brothers in the monastery were soon astounded by the young man. His humility and acts of charity were unsurpassed, and he began to have visions and go into ecstatic trances that were seen as clear signs of divine favor. Nine years after entering the monastery, his superiors asked him to become a full religious, and as the years passed his fellow brothers looked to him as their spiritual leader. Through all this, Martin retained his humility; he often referred to himself as a "poor slave" or a "mulatto dog."

Like **St. Francis of Assisi** (see no. 34),

Martin had an amazing way with animals. Many stories have been told about his ability to communicate with all types of animals; the most remarkable is the tale of how he persuaded some mice to stop taking from the monastery's stores. (He then fed the mice from his own portions.) Stories were also told of Martin's ability to "bilocate," meaning that he could be in two places at one time. As these stories spread, so did his fame, and in his lifetime Martin became the best-known spiritual leader in South America.

Martin foretold the day and hour of his death. He passed away happily at the age of 60, after apologizing to his fellows for what he called the "poor example" he had often set. His funeral was attended by the Archbishop of Mexico and the Viceroy of Peru. He was *canonized* by Pope **John XXIII** in 1962, and he is the patron saint of social and interracial justice.

A Catholic church in Lima, Peru

61. Anne Hutchinson
(1591–1643)

One of the earliest fighters for religious freedom in the American colonies was an Englishwoman who defied Boston's *Puritan* elders to speak out for her beliefs.

Born at Alford, England in 1591, **Anne Marbury** was the daughter of a minister in the *Anglican church*. She married William Hutchinson, a merchant, in 1612, and the couple eventually had 14 children.

The Hutchinson family emigrated to Boston, **Massachusetts** in 1634. Anne became a valued member of the community, especially noted for her skill in herbal medicine. Soon after the family's arrival, she began to hold prayer meetings at her home; the meetings grew into discussions and interpretations of the Sunday sermons given by Reverend John Cotton.

Anne Hutchinson

Anne became the leading member of the congregants who believed in a "covenant of grace" rather than a "covenant of works." This meant that they believed that God's grace was large enough to allow each person to make his or her own peace with God, rather than having to rely upon the help of a minister or priest. It was a debate that went back to Martin Luther's formation of the Lutheran church during the 1520s.

So spirited was the discussion that about 60 people became regular members of the meetings; one of them was Sir **Henry Vane**, governor of the colony. At first, Hutchinson had some support within the community, and some protection, from powerful figures such as Vane. However, eventually things turned against her. **John Winthrop**, a former—and future—governor was alarmed by Hutchinson's leadership of the meetings. There were no women ministers among the Puritans; who did this woman think she was?

In 1637, Vane left the colony; in August that year, at the first *synod* of the Puritan church, Hutchinson was denounced for daring to take a position of leadership. In November, she was summoned to appear before a special council held just outside of Boston. She was charged with *antinomianism*; found guilty by the council, she was banished from the colony.

Hutchinson and her family went to the **Rhode Island** colony, founded by Roger Williams. Her husband died in 1642, and the following year, she moved with her family to a section of **Long Island** controlled by the Dutch. There she hoped to find peace.

In 1643, Anne Hutchinson and most of her family were killed in an Indian raid. Boston's Puritan leaders rejoiced; they claimed that her death was a sign that God disapproved of her former actions. To Americans who believe in the religious freedom, she was and remains one of the leading lights of that cause. A statue of her stands near the State House in Boston.

62. George Fox
(1624–1691)

They call themselves the Religious Society of Friends, however, most people call them **Quakers**. Their founder was **George Fox**.

Born in Leicestershire, England in 1624, Fox was the son of *Puritan* parents. As a young boy, he was an apprentice to a cobbler. In September 1643, at the age of 19, Fox experienced a call to forsake all his family, friends, and associations. He left his work and home and wandered for some time, seeking another religious experience. In 1647, when he was close to giving up entirely, Fox reportedly heard a voice that said, "There is one, even Christ Jesus, that can speak to thy condition."

Fox's heart leapt for joy; this was the direct revelation he had been seeking. From that time onward, he spoke and wrote of the "Christ Within or the **Inner Light**," which became the centerpiece of Quaker doctrine. Fox preached that God spoke directly to people, as he had in Biblical times. Salvation was an individual matter between a person and God; this inner voice or light was to guide a person, more than even the Bible or the church. Therefore, it followed, there was no need for ministers or priests.

This doctrine was unlike nearly all Christian sects of the time. Both Anglicans and Puritans disliked Fox's ideas and actively persecuted him.

However, by the early 1650s, Fox had brought together many converts. He sent them to spread the Quaker faith to Ireland, Scotland, Wales, European countries, Russia, Turkey, and the English colonies in North America, where Fox traveled in 1672 and 1673.

Most converts to the Quaker faith were of lower or middle class origin. An important exception was **Margaret Fell**, mistress of Swarthmoor Hall and the widow of a member of Parliament. She gave generous assistance to the Quaker cause and in 1669, she and Fox were married.

George Fox preaching

Although he preferred not to organize his followers, Fox found it necessary to provide some structure to the new faith. The yearly Quaker meetings became a tradition. By the time of his death in 1691, Fox had created a new religion, one that maintained a great belief in the worth and dignity of each individual. Women and men were equals in the Society of Friends. Converts like **William Penn** and **John Woolman** brought the faith to America, where it took strongest root in **Philadelphia** and **New Jersey**.

Throughout their history, the Quakers have preached **pacifism**, and they were actively involved in the movement to abolish slavery in all English-speaking countries during the 18th and 19th centuries.

Emanuel Swedenborg

Emanuel Swedenborg was a Swedish scientist and philosopher who became a *mystic* at the age of 55, and devoted the rest of his life to spiritualism.

He was born in Stockholm in 1688, the son of Jasper Svedberg, a Lutheran bishop.(In 1719, the family was ennobled and took the name Swendenborg.) After graduating from the University of Uppsala, the young man became an official with the Swedish Board of Mines, specializing in geology and military engineering.

Swedenborg became a first-rate scientist and mathematician. He published several papers on algebra and decimals, as well as works on astronomical observations of the moon and the planets, and ocean depths and the force of tides. His most important scientific writing is the three-volume *Opera Philisophica Et Mineralia*. All the science known in his day can be found in his writings, as well as his own discoveries and advanced theories.

In 1734, at the age of 46, he turned away from the physical sciences to perform pioneer work in the areas of philosophy and psychology. He also became engaged in thoughts about the theory of creation, and set forth his ideas in two works: *The Infinite, and the Final Cause of Creation*, and *The Intercourse Between the Soul and the Body*.

In 1745, Swedenborg claimed to have received a vision of the spiritual world. By 1747, he had abandoned all his earlier work in other areas, and for the rest of his life he wrote numerous volumes about his continuing visions and spiritual discoveries. His best known work is *Heaven and Hell*, which describes his travels in the spiritual spheres. He also wrote new interpretations of Biblical symbols and correspondences.

Swedenborg described three spheres of existence—**Divine Mind**, **Spiritual World** and **Natural World**. All three are bound together by what he called **Correspondences**—real connections deeper than symbolism. Unlike many other mystics, Swedenborg taught an approach to God and Spirit through the natural world, rather than through avoidance of it.

In his personal life Swedenborg was charming and very sociable. He lived a simple life as a vegetarian, and often remained in trances for days at a time. He never married, and when asked why, he explained that his soul mate awaited him in Heaven.

Though he remained a devout Christian, Swedenborg began to criticize Protestant theology. Gradually, his writings, such as *The New Jerusalem* and *The True Christian Religion*, aroused the anger of the Lutheran clergy. Eventually, he was forced to leave Sweden; he went to England, where he died in 1772.

Although Swedenborg never attempted to founded his own new church, six years after his death, his followers founded the Church of the New Jerusalem, or **Swedenborgians**, which is still active today.

64. Baal Shem Tov (Besht)
(c. 1700–1760)

The founder of the branch of **Judaism** known as **Hasidism, Israel ben Eliezer** was born in the village of Okup in the Polish **Ukraine** around 1700. Even as a young man, people recognized his warm, magnetic personality.

Eliezer married early, and he and his wife spent several years living in poverty in the Carpathian Mountains in present-day Hungary. At 36, he emerged from years of solitude and announced that he had become a faith healer and exorcist. He traveled through the villages, healing people with herbal remedies, amulets, and prayers. Like other amulet makers, he claimed to be weaving elements of God's name into the device; therefore he became known as **Baal Shem Tov**, or "Master of the Good Name." Some people put the initials together into an acronym and called him the "Besht."

While wandering in the mountains, Baal Shem Tov developed a set of beliefs that were essentially *pantheistic*. The essence of his philosophy was that God is present in all living things, whether they seem evil or good to us in the present moment. In the last 20 years of his life, he laid down the elements of his beliefs, what came to be called Hasidism, a **mystical strain** of Judaism.

The core elements were joyfulness, fervent prayer, and observance of the **Ten Commandments**—all leading to an emotional, rather than a rational, attachment to God. Most important, this new brand of Judaism allowed for joyful engagement by all Jews, unlike the study of *Talmud* in which only the learned could participate. Baal Shem Tov taught his followers that feeling the presence of God was not reserved for the mystical elite; all Jews had a duty to practice *devekuth*—a discipline of concentration—and in doing so could experience ecstatic joy. There were also aspects of folk healing in Hasidism; some of Baal Shem Tov's homeopathic remedies have survived until today.

The most controversial aspect was that Baal Shem Tov required his followers to rely on their *Zaddick*, a holy man (in this case, him), who was to be the intermediary between God and the Chosen People.

A joyful celebration of God

Baal Shem Tov did not write down his teachings, and he forbade his followers to do so. Twenty years after his death in 1760, **Jacob Joseph**, one of his disciples, published hundreds of Baal Shem Tov's sermons and homilies.

Baal Shem Tov had formed a core group of devoted followers who spread his teachings throughout **Poland** and the Ukraine. Within the next generation a large number of the Jews in those areas became followers of Hasidism.

The founder of **Methodism** was born at Epworth, in Lincolnshire, England in 1703. His parents were devout Anglicans.

John Wesley graduated from Christ Church at Oxford, and continued his studies under a fellowship. He was *ordained* in the *Anglican church* in 1728. Wesley experienced something which was reported by many members of his generation. They felt the church had become dry and formal; there was little emotional enthusiasm. Wesley never intended to create a new church, but he wanted to bring life back to the faith of his parents.

John Wesley

In 1735, Wesley and his younger brother **Charles** went as missionaries to the new colony of Georgia in North America, to convert the colonists and the Native Americans. Their joint ministry there was a failure, but Wesley was deeply impressed by the quiet faith of the German Moravian settlers, whom he met on board the ship to the New World.

In 1738, the brothers returned to England; soon both of them underwent conversion experiences. On Wednesday, May 24, while at a Moravian service in London, John Wesley experienced a vivid personal awakening: "I felt my heart strangely warmed. I felt I did trust in Christ, Christ alone for salvation"

From that day forth, Wesley became a true **evangelist**. After spending a short time in Germany, he began his "field preaching" on April 2, 1739 in Bristol, England with 3,000 people in attendance. Soon, he was preaching everywhere—in local churches, on the streets, and at public gatherings. Before long, Wesley was able to report that the apathy he had often experienced in formal church gatherings was being offset by the energy created by his vigorous preaching.

Wesley ignored the Anglican establishment, which was critical of his emphasis on personal salvation through faith alone. So, while he and his followers remained Anglicans in theory, his methods and organizational plans eventually led to the formation of the new Methodist church.

Wesley's established a unique structure for his growing movement; he organized his converts into "societies." Each society was in turn divided into "classes," with "class leaders" who attended to the spiritual needs of individual members. Each of the classes also had "stewards" who handled their financial concerns. By 1744, the movement had grown so much, that Wesley called the first annual conference in London to address issues of governance of the societies.

During the 1760s and 1770s, Wesley became deeply involved in the pursuit of **social justice**. He pioneered efforts in legal and prison reform, and campaigned vigorously for the abolition of British participation in the slave trade. He died in 1791, leaving behind a remarkable record of evangelism and preaching on behalf of the social gospel.

66. George Whitefield
1714–1770

One of the most famous spiritual leaders and evangelists of the American colonial period, **George Whitefield** was born in Gloucester, England. Although many of his ancestors had been clergymen, George's own father was an innkeeper. By his early teens George was already a pious Christian, and when he went to Oxford in 1732, he came under the influence of Charles and **John Wesley**, the founders of Methodism (see no. 65).

The transforming moment of Whitefield's life came during an illness in 1735, when he was filled with a sense of oneness with God and experienced what he called a "new birth." From that point on, he would work to convince others that such an experience was vital to becoming a true Christian. In that sense, he was the founder of "**born again" Christianity**.

Whitefield soon embarked on the career that would make him famous, a life of constant preaching in any available site, as well as a humanitarian who ministered to the poor. As an evangelical preacher, he was quite unlike most clergymen of his time; he employed the voice and manner of an actor to excite his audience. Because he did not conform to the teachings of the established Church of England, he would spend the rest of his long career under attack from conventional Christians.

In 1738, Whitefield made his first trip to America, landing at Savannah, Georgia, which was then a new colony. Here he began his preaching in the colonies, and started the first of his numerous endeavors to found orphanages and schools. The following year, the **Great Awakening** religious movement began, and Whitefield became one of its most prominent leaders. Whitefield's preaching represented the more outward and emotional forms of the Awakening, while its somber and scholarly aspects were presented by Reverend **Jonathan Edwards**.

For the next 30 years, Whitefield traveled back and forth frequently between England and the colonies. Whenever he was in America, he moved up and down the Eastern seaboard giving hundreds of sermons. Whitefield was not an easy person to satisfy or get along with. He became increasingly more rigid in his religious views, and he quarreled not only with other colonial clergymen, but even with John Wesley, the Methodist who had first inspired him. Whitefield was also a man of his time in that while he advocated the humane treatment of slaves, he saw nothing wrong in owning some on his plantation in South Carolina.

Whitefield was a man of extraordinary energy whose preaching engaged people from all walks of life. He died in Newburyport, Massachusetts, near the end of one of his frequent tours of the colonies.

George Whitefield

67. Elijah ben Solomon
(1720–1797)

Some spiritual leaders lead through inspiration and charisma. Others, such as **Elijah ben Solomon**, use their profound learning to influence others.

Elijah ben Solomon was born in Selec, Lithuania in 1720. Even as a young boy he showed his extraordinary intellect; he was able to study the Bible and the Talmud by himself at the age of six. One year later he was brought to **Vilna**, to study with the most learned rabbis in Eastern Europe. He sometimes astounded his teachers, coming to conclusions so quickly that they could not follow the train of his thought.

At 18, Elijah married Hannah, a rabbi's daughter. From the ages of 20 to 28, he traveled by himself through many of the kingdoms of Europe, seeing first-hand how Jews lived in those countries. When he returned to Vilna, he declined to become a rabbi; he preferred the freedom he had as a lay person.

Because of his wife's devotion and a family trust fund, Elijah was able to devote all his time and energy to study of the *Talmud* and *Torah*. To avoid distractions, he shut the windows of his room by day and studied by candlelight. He sometimes slept only two hours a night because he was possessed by such a great desire for learning. By the time he was in his forties, Elijah had become the Gaon—or head—of the academy

Elijah ben Solomon

of Vilna, and the unofficial leader of Jews in Eastern Europe. Many questions and issues were brought to his attention for judgment.

Elijah faced a profound dilemma during the last 30 years of his life. Many Eastern European Jews had become members of the **Hasidim**, a sect that emphasized an individual's emotional attachment to God through fervent prayer and reliance on a *Zaddick* (holy man). Elijah was strongly opposed to this group. He became the spokesperson for traditional Jewish ways and a rational attachment to God, based on adherence to the Torah and Talmud. He denounced the Hasidic leader **Baal Shem Tov** (see no. 64) and others as charlatans, and was especially opposed to the concept of the *Zaddick*. Elijah saw this as just old-fashioned idol worship. Some other rabbis were inclined to go easy on the Hasidim, but Elijah announced that "all those who follow this path never return—it is heresy.

Around 1783, Elijah acted upon his lifelong dream of seeing Erez Israel (the Jewish name for the Holy Land). He set out on his journey, but had to turn back; history does not record what prevented him from reaching his destination.

Elijah wrote about 70 books during his lifetime. He also trained and educated a large number of disciples to carry on his teachings.

A German philosopher and Jewish leader was responsible for helping Jews leave their ghettos and integrate into European society during Europe's great period of **Enlightenment**.

Moses Mendelssohn was born in Dessau, Germany—then part of the Holy Roman Empire. The son of a poor *Torah* scribe, he received his early education from his father, but went to Berlin in 1743 to undertake more secular studies.

At the time, the intellectual phenomenon that came to be called the Enlightenment was then in full swing; important literature, periodicals, and newspapers were being published, and well-educated people throughout Europe believed that they were coming closer and closer to the truth about the world and mankind's place in it. In Berlin, Mendelssohn became exposed to this movement, and his home became a gathering place for Berlin intellectuals. What was so remarkable about this was that Mendelssohn was a Jew; at the time, most Jews lived in ghettos and had little contact with gentiles in society other than for commercial ventures.

Mendelssohn steeped himself in the literature of the time. He read John Locke, William Shaftesbury, Gottfried Liebniz, and Christian Wolff. From all of these thinkers, he gained the belief that the time had come for religious tolerance, communication between different religious groups, freedom of conscience, and the separation of church and state.

Phadon, on the Immortality of the Soul, Mendelssohn's first book, was published in 1767. A defense of the notion of the immortality of the soul, he demonstrated that man had a will and being that was superior to anything he might experience in the world. Mendelssohn also translated the Pentateuch (the first five books of the Old Testament) into German; this was published in 1780. Then came *Morning Hours, or Lectures on the Existence of God,* published in 1785. In that book, Mendelssohn described a philosophical God, a Supreme Being that could possess human characteristics such as wisdom, goodness, justice, and intellect.

In other writings, Mendelssohn argued for freedom of conscience in religion and a **separation of Church and State**. He stated that Jewish religious law is binding only on Jews, but their adherence to this law should not prevent them from becoming loyal citizens of any state. What surprised his readers was that Mendelssohn, raised in a traditional Jewish family, was able to incorporate his ideas and beliefs and present them to a wider audience, that of the Enlightenment.

Mendelssohn died in 1786. During that same decade, a number of his intellectual disciples became leaders in the new **Haskalah**, the Jewish form of the Enlightenment.

A medal in honor of Mendelssohn

Mendelssohn's important contributions enabled Jews to live both in the modern world and still abide by the faithful traditions of their past.

The Shakers at worship

Ann Lee, the founder and leader of the Shaker faith, was born in Manchester, England in 1736, the daughter of a blacksmith. When she was in her early 20s, she met Jane and James Wardley, the leaders of a new Christian sect called the "Shaking Quakers," a group of Quakers (see no. 62) so nicknamed because they shook violently while undergoing spiritual experiences. The Wardleys believed that on Christ's Second Coming to Earth, he would appear as a woman. Ann became their strongest convert, and as her faith grew, the Wardleys became convinced that she was the Second Coming.

Ann married Abraham Stanley, a blacksmith, in 1762. She had four difficult births, and each of her children died in infancy. These severe losses pushed Ann toward her belief in a religion that would forswear sex and marriage.

In the early 1770s, Ann Lee decided to emigrate to America. She, her husband, her brother William, her niece, and five other Shaking Quakers, sailed for New York City in 1774. Ann's marriage ended in New York, and she retained her maiden name. In 1776, she and her small group of followers moved up the Hudson River and founded the first Shaker colony at Watervliet, New York, which they soon called "**Wisdom Valley**."

At Watervliet, "Mother" Ann set down the rules for her colony and faith. The Shaking Quakers, or Shakers as others began to call them, practiced a strict lifestyle. All followers were to abstain from drinking alcohol. Men and women were completely separated except during times of worship. There were different houses, sets of rooms, and even two different stairways that led to the common area where they met for prayer. In addition, complete celibacy was practiced. Mother Ann had become convinced that the world would soon come to an end, therefore there was no point in furthering the population. Despite this rigid lifestyle, the Shakers sang and danced regularly, and all their work was devoted to creating a harmonious and simple manner of life.

In May, 1780, Mother Ann believed she received a sign to begin her **evangelism**. She and a handful of other Shakers went on a tour of New England that lasted for two years and four months. Among the few converts she made was **Joseph Meacham**, who continued her work after her death in 1784.

The Shaker faith blossomed during the 19th century. Thousands of Americans joined Shaker communities in New England and New York. During this time, Shakers became noted for their **architectural designs**, which were considered some of the most efficient and quietly elegant of all American building types. The Shakers also invented the circular barn and certain types of brooms.

St. Seraphim of Sarov
(1759–1833)

The Russian people converted to Orthodox Christianity shortly after A.D. 1000. In the centuries that followed, devout Russians added a new aspect to their Orthodox faith—that of the *starets*, or holy man. One of the most notable of these men was **Seraphim of Sarov**.

Born in Kursk in 1759, his given name was **Prokhor Moshnin**. His father was a prominent brick-maker and builder who died in 1760, while he was building the Kazan Church of the *icon* of the Mother of God. The third child in the family, in his youth Prokhor helped to finish the church. Then he left Kursk to join the monastery of Sarov, in the province of Tambov.

Prokhor arrived at Sarov on December 2, 1778. He entered the *novitiate* and was *ordained* a priest in 1793. From the beginning, he was an unusual monk; he preferred rough garments to smooth ones, and seemed immune to bodily discomforts. On December 2, 1794, exactly 16 years after his entry, he asked permission to become a *hermit* in a hut three miles outside the monastery. Permission was granted.

Prokhor dug a stone chamber out of the granite on which the hut was built. The chamber was big enough for him either to stand up or lie down. Soon he began an ordeal of 1,000 days and nights of prayer, on his knees, on the granite floor.

When he emerged from this period, Prokhor was a changed man. Where before he had been knowledgeable, now he was wise. Before he had been caring and gentle, now he was truly holy. The light of personal revelation shone in his face, and people came from far and wide to seek his counsel.

About this same time, Prokhor began to be known as Seraphim of Sarov. He was now a *starets*, a holy man in the **Russian Orthodox** tradition, one who has received his learning both from books and from the natural world. However, even as his fame spread beyond Sarov, Seraphim underwent criticism from his fellow monks, many of whom believed he was not humble enough, and that he should live a more ordinary life, in union with them.

In 1804, Seraphim was attacked and wounded by robbers; he spent the rest of his life weakened from the assault. From 1807 to 1810, Seraphim underwent a period of complete silence and isolation in his hermitage. When he "came back to Sarov" and the world, people flocked to see him. During the decade of the 1820s, he was the most sought-after spiritual counselor in Russia.

Seraphim of Sarov was *canonized* on August 1, 1903, in a ceremony attended by Czar Nicholas II and Czarina Alexandra.

St. Basil's Orthodox Church in Moscow

71. Innokentii Veniaminov
(1797–1879)

While 18th and 19th century French and Spanish priests sought to convert Native Americans to Catholicism, the **Aleut Indians** of southern **Alaska** were converted to the **Russian Orthodox** church, largely through the efforts of one man.

John Popov Veniaminov was born in Anga, near Irkutsk, Siberia in 1797. The son of a local church official, he graduated from the seminary at Irkutsk in 1818. He married, and showed every sign of living an average life in his homeland.

Then came a call for priests to go to Alaska, at the time a Russian territory, and convert the natives who lived on the Aleutian Islands. Veniaminov felt called to this work; he, his wife, brother, and mother undertook a 14-month journey that brought them to Unalaska among the Aleutian Islands.

Innokentii Veniaminov

First, Veniaminov built a house and church. Then he learned the Aleut language and created a written alphabet. His first book, *A Guide to the Way to the Heavenly Kingdom*, was written in the Aleut language. It was later translated into Russian and went into 46 editions. Aside from his spiritual calling, Veniaminov was an amateur scientist and anthropologist; his *Notes on the Islands of the Unalaska District* ran to three volumes and is still used by scientists and historians.

After 10 years among the Aleut, Veniaminov was transferred to Sitka, Alaska, where he worked for four years among the **Tlingit Indians**. After this, he went home to Russia, to arrange for the publication of his writings. Soon after his return home, his wife died. Veniaminov entered a monastic order and changed his name to Innokentii. However, his days in North America were far from over.

In 1840, the Russian Orthodox Church created a new Diocese of North America and Kamchatka. Veniaminov became its first bishop. He returned to Sitka in 1841 and spent the next nine years as an active evangelist, traveling through southern Alaska, bringing Christianity to the native peoples there. In 1850, the diocese was enlarged, and he became an archbishop.

Veniaminov received the highest possible honor in 1868, when he was made **metropolitan** (senior archbishop) of Moscow. He returned to Russia, and in 1870 he established the **Orthodox Missionary Society**; his goal was to convince every member of the church to spread the Orthodox Christian word—and he was successful. Russian missionaries founded churches from the Altai Mountains in Central Asia to China and Japan. Veniaminov's associate Nikolai Kassatkin followed his example; he went to Japan, learned the Japanese language, and started a Japanese branch of the Russian church.

Veniaminov died in 1879. He was *canonized* in 1977, and given the title, Evangelizer of the Aleut and **Apostle to America**.

72. Joseph Smith
(1805–1844)

The founder of **Mormonism** was a small-town farm boy from New England.

The fourth of ten children, **Joseph Smith** was born in Sharon, Vermont in 1805. His family moved to western New York State in 1816, and settled in what was called the "Burned-Over District," so-called because many fire-and-brimstone preachers had passed through the area. Perhaps the location affected Smith, for between 1824 and 1830 he established the first religion to originate in America after the birth of the country.

Smith later claimed he was visited by an angel named Moroni on a hillside near Palmyra, New York. Smith said he had the first of his visions in 1820; they were followed by others on September 21 and 22, 1823. In 1827, the angel led Smith to a set of golden plates, long buried in the countryside. Smith translated and transcribed the plates, and on April 6, 1830 he announced the formation of the *Church of Latter-Day Saints of Jesus Christ.*

That same year Smith's writings were published as the **Book of Mormon**. The book explained that the Native Americans were descendants of a Hebrew named Nephi and his family, who had belonged to one of the Lost Tribes of ancient Israel. It was now Smith's assignment to gather the lost peoples and create a new Zion (Israel) in North America. The Book of Mormon capitalized on the interest of many Americans in the origins of the **Native Americans**, and Smith began to win converts.

Smith led a group of followers to Kirtland, Ohio, then to Jackson County, Missouri, and finally to Commerce, Illinois which he renamed **Nauvoo**. They built a great temple there, and the population of Nauvoo reached 15,000, making it the largest town in Illinois.

By 1844, Smith had become the most successful leader of a "fringe" religion anywhere

Joseph Smith

in the United States. He had also attracted the envy and distrust of many non-Mormons, especially when rumors spread that Smith and other Mormon leaders were practicing **polygamy**.

In 1844, Smith announced that he was a candidate for president of the United States. This caused his enemies to plot against him, and he was arrested and brought to the jail at Carthage, Illinois. There he was murdered by an angry mob.

Rather than bringing the Mormon experiment to an end, Smith's death became a catalyst for another move—and its ultimate growth. In 1847, **Brigham Young** brought the Mormons to the **Great Salt Lake** in present-day Utah. The Mormons thrived there, and when Utah joined the union, the Mormon Church remained the most powerful influence within that state. Smith's vision had come to pass.

In the early 19th century, a self-proclaimed prophet established the **Bahai faith**—which preached a "unity of mankind" and a unity of all religions.

Baha' Allah was born **Mirza Husayn Ali Nuri**, in Tehran, the capital of Persia, in 1817. During the 1840s he became a follower of the movement known as "the **Babis**," who followed the Bab, or "Gate" to the truth. The Bab, whose birth name was Mirza Ali Muhammad of Shiraz (1819-1850), claimed that he was a prophet, making the way for "he whom God shall manifest," and therefore played a role similar to that of John the Baptist for Christians.

In 1850, supporters of the Bab were involved in a rebellion against the Perisan authorities, and he was executed; as a follower of the Bab, Baha' Allah was put in a Tehran prison. Released in 1853, he was banished to Baghdad, and then banished a second time, to Istanbul, center of the Ottoman Empire. Shortly before he left Baghdad, in April 1863, Baha' Allah announced to his friends and followers that he was the prophet whom the Bab had described. From then on, he was known as Baha' Allah ("Splendor of God"), and many of the supporters of the Bab followed him.

After a brief stay in Turkey, Baha' Allah was exiled to Palestine. He was imprisoned in Acre for nine years; during that time he wrote *Kitab al-Aqdas* (*Book of the Most Holy*). Baha' Allah's message incorporated the teachings of other religions which had originated in the Middle East. According to the book, God is both unknowable and inaccessible (like the God of the burning bush, as revealed to Moses), but he sends messengers who are known as divine manifestations. Among these were Zoroaster, Abraham, Moses, Jesus, and Muhammad.

Unity of God, **unity of religion**, and the **unity of mankind** is the central message of Baha' Allah's teaching. Each of the divine manifestations rose to a higher level than the previous ones, because he spoke and preached to a greater level of unity. Baha' Allah was in the line of divine manifestation, but he did not claim that he was the last of the prophets. Equality of men and women, and harmony between science and religion were other key elements of the Bahai faith.

Released from prison, Baha' Allah spent his last years at his home near Haifa in present-day Israel. He died there in 1892. By then, the Bahai faith had spread to Europe and the United States. Leadership of the Bahai passed to Baha' Allah's son, **Abd al-Baha**, who died in 1921; in his will, he passed the leadership on to his oldest grandson. Today there are more than five million followers of the faith.

Abd al-Baha, 1912

Mary Morse Baker was born in Bow, New Hampshire in 1821, the sixth and last child in the family. Her father was a strict *Protestant*; her mother had a more open and embracing Protestant faith.

Mary Baker married George Washington Glover, a builder and contractor from South Carolina, in 1843. He died the next year after a brief illness. She was married a second time, to Daniel Patterson, a dentist, in 1853. Although they remained legally married for 20 years, it was an unfortunate union, and appears to have had little positive impact on her life.

For more than a decade during her 30s, Mary Patterson suffered from numerous ailments, which could not be properly diagnosed. She was confined to her bed for months at a time, and often had to be carried from place to place. Her only relief came in 1862, when she visited the itinerant healer **Phineas Quimby** (1802-1866) in Portland, Maine. Through a process of hand-healing and hypnotism, Quimby brought her immediate relief from pain.

On February 1, 1866, Mary Patterson fell on an icy street; she suffered a concussion and severely injured her spine. Bedridden, she read the Biblical account of Jesus' healing a man with palsy. She claimed she underwent a spiritual experience in which God spoke to her and said, "Daughter, arise!" Her pain disappeared; she got up, dressed herself, and walked into her living room, shocking her friends, who believed she way dying. Thus began her ministry in the cause of **Christian Science**.

Like Quimby before her, Mary Patterson was convinced that all illnesses and diseases had mental, rather than physical, origins. Therefore, she and a growing number of followers emphasized the importance of right-mindedness, which meant opening to the love and healing offered by God.

Mary Patterson published *Science and Health with Key to the Scriptures* in 1875. The book was reissued 382 times during her lifetime. Two years later she married Asa Gilbert Eddy, a sewing-machine salesman, and acquired the last name which is most familiar to her followers. The **Church of Christ, Scientist**, was chartered in 1879. It was the start of a new religion that had no clergy, but was defined by an indescribable trust in the wisdom and mercy of God.

Mary Baker Eddy

In 1881, she founded the **Massachusetts Metaphysical College**, which taught courses in Pathology, Ontology, and Moral Science, and their application to the treatment of diseases. Before the end of the decade, there were 30 more such colleges throughout the United States. In 1908, Eddy founded the *Christian Science Monitor*, which remains one of the most respected periodicals in the United States. Since Eddy's death in 1910, the Christian Science Church has grown and flourished.

75. Helena Petrovna Blavatsky
(1831–1891)

During the last third of the 19th century, a remarkable and eccentric woman helped reawaken Hindus to their spiritual heritage, and made Eastern spirituality extremely popular in the United States and Western Europe.

Helena de Hahn was born in Ekaterinoslav, Ukraine in 1831. Her father was a prominent aristocrat; her mother was a successful novelist. In 1849, Helena married Nikifor Blavatsky, the vice-governor of a city in Russian Armenia. She left him before the honeymoon had ended, and went on her own to Constantinople.

Helena Blavatsky spent the next 24 years constantly traveling. She journeyed to England, the United States, India, southern Russia, and the Caucasus Mountains. The most controversial of her claims, which was never verified, is that she lived in Tibet and was initiated into secret religious lineages there.

In 1873, she went to New York City, where she met **Henry Steel Olcott** (1832-1907), a journalist who was interested in the occult. On November 17, 1875, they co-founded the **Theosophical Society**, a religious movement that rejected the traditional Judaeo-Christian and Islamic doctrines, emphasizing instead **Indian Eastern spiritualism**, as well as **occultism** and **Egyptology**.

Though she had little formal schooling, Madame Blavatsky (as she was generally called) was a formidable writer. She published *Isis Unveiled* in 1877, and *The Secret Doctrine* in 1888. Both books won tremendous praise from her devotees, and some severe criticism from other quarters. Her critics complained that while her books displayed her considerable knowledge of Eastern spirituality, they provided no formula for the reader to follow in his or her own spiritual quest.

Blavatsky and Olcott left the United States in 1879 and went to India. They settled in Bombay, and in 1882 they purchased an estate at Adyar, near Madras. From their home, the two embarked on a program of reawakening Hindus to their own spiritual heritage, something that naturally brought them both praise and vilification. In 1885, Blavatsky left India for Europe, while Olcott continued their work in India.

Blavatsky died in London in 1891. The *New York Daily Tribune* saluted her in the following manner: "No one in the present generation, it may be said, has done more toward reopening the long sealed treasures of Eastern thought, wisdom, and philosophy."

By the late 19th century, leadership of the Theosophical movement in India passed to **Annie Besant** (1847–1933). Under her direction, the movement continued the reawakening of Hindu spiritualism begun by Blavatsky, and established educational institutions emphasizing Theosophical curriculum.

Helena Blavatsky

76. Ramakrishna
(1836–1886)

Kali is the *Hindu* goddess of destruction and transformation. Depictions of her swirling arms bring a sense of terror to the uninitiated, but to leaders such as **Ramakrishna**, she was the Divine Mother who renews life through the presence of death.

Gadadhar Chatterjee was born in the Bengalese village of Kamarpukur in 1836. As a child, he experienced spiritual raptures prompted by the sights and wonders of the natural world. After the death of his father, Chatterjee followed his older brother to Calcutta, where he served as a priest in a temple devoted to the **worship of Kali**. Chatterjee became his brother's assistant, and when the brother died in 1856, Chatterjee took his place. He also took the religious name Ramakrishna.

By his own admission, Ramakrishna became "perfectly insane" for a year or two. He went in and out of trances, came close to death, and was completely absorbed in his uncharted spiritual journey. To restore himself, he sought the counsel of people more spiritually advanced than himself.

A middle-aged woman named Yogesvari was the first of his teachers. She instructed him in the **Tantric disciplines** that emphasize the meeting point between spirituality and sexuality. Some Tantric practices call for a complete abandonment to sensual pleasure, while others emphasize the contain- ment, or bottling up, or

Ramakrishna

spiritual energies, until they can be released in a moment of choice. In either case, the point is to use sexuality as a bridge toward one's own spiritual nature.

Next came a man named Totapuri. He instructed Ramakrishna in the mind-science of absolute nondualism. Like many Eastern leaders, Totapuri believed that a spiritual seek- er had to go beyond any and all forms— including God— and reach the nameless and formless presence that lies behind them all.

After Totapuri, Ramakrishna became his own leader and guru to many other seekers. He returned to the direct worship of Kali, see- ing in her the Divine Mother who brings death to everything, yet in doing so clears the way for rebirth. Ramakrishna's disciples often saw him in the midst of *samadhi,* a trancelike absorption into the essence of God.

Seeking to know more about other faiths, Ramakrishna spent four days absorbed in a meditation on Muhammad and emerged saying that he had experi- enced the essence of Allah. A similar trance yielded him access to the essence of Jesus Christ. These meditations produced such intense visions of God, similar to all his Hindu experiences, that Ramakrishna became con- vinced of the ultimate unity of all religions.

Ramakrishna died in 1886, having brought about a major resurgence in Hindu worship, especially among the intellec- tuals of Calcutta. His disciple **Swami Vivekananda** (see no. 79) spread his gospel to other parts of the world.

Dwight Lyman Moody
(1837–1899)

By the middle of the 19th century, American *Protestant* church leaders began to worry about the lack of energy in their congregations. It was especially true in the urban churches, but even rural pastors wondered how to bring faith and fervor to their flocks. **Dwight Lyman Moody** was the answer to their prayers.

The son of a bricklayer, Moody was born in Northfield, Massachusetts in 1837. He had only an elementary school education, and he never obtained any formal religious training. At the age of 17, he went to Boston where he worked as a shoe salesman. In 1856, Moody moved on to Chicago, which was the growing hub of the American Midwest. He married Emma Revell in 1862, and the couple eventually had three children.

Moody's career in public service blossomed at the end of the Civil War. He became president of the Chicago branch of the Young Men's Christian Association **(YMCA)** in 1866, and he was very active in city affairs. Then came the Great Chicago Fire of 1871,

Dwight Lyman Moody

which destroyed both the YMCA building and the Congregationalist church that Moody attended. Around that time, Moody underwent a personal spiritual conversion that made his religious experience much more immediate and personal.

In 1873, Moody took advantage of an opportunity to go to England and Scotland as an evangelical preacher, seeking to bring people to God. He stayed abroad for two years, and the bricklayer's son and shoe salesman demonstrated a remarkable capacity for finding converts. When he returned to the United States in 1875, he had become the most popular **revivalist preacher** in the country, a position he held until his death. It added to his fame that he had earned his stripes, so to speak, in a foreign country.

Moody was not an intellectual, or even a deep thinker. He had what was essentially a middle-class American approach to religion; he didn't have a reasoned or defined theology. He wore dark business suits when he preached, and his use of a choir was important in making music more of a force in American religion.

Moody returned to Northfield in 1875 and made his hometown the base of his operations. Between 1879 and 1881, he founded the Northfield Seminary for female students and the Mount Hermon School for males; they later merged into the **Northfield Mount Hermon School**. He also founded the **Chicago Bible Institute** in 1886, which specialized in training evangelists for city congregations, and inspired the creation of two Christian publishing companies. By the time of his death, Moody had preached to an estimated 100 million people, and had spurred a strong evangelical movement that sent out thousands of young missionaries around the country.

A European scholar who aspired to bring humankind back to a golden era, developed a "scientific" religious movement in the early 20th century.

Rudolf Steiner was born in Kraljevic, in present-day Croatia in 1861. His father was a minor railroad official; his mother was a peasant woman. Steiner attributed much of his success to being raised by loving parents, and having the good fortune of growing up in beautiful physical surroundings.

After studying natural science at Vienna University, Steiner went to live in Weimar, Germany. There he edited the scientific works of **Johann Wolfgang von Goethe**, whose philosophies had a major influence upon his development. By the time Steiner published *Die Philosophie der Freiheit* (*The Philosophy of Freedom*) in 1894, Steiner appeared to be leading the life of an average, successful academic. This book, and the many others that followed showed he was anything but average—Steiner was in fact a profound *mystic* who had come to his mysticism without any formal religious training.

In the early years of the 20th century, Steiner became involved with the German section of the **Theosophical Society**, the movement begun by Helena Blavatsky (see no. 75) in 1875. Steiner was a follower of theosophism for about 10 years, when in 1912, he decided to break away and found his own movement which came to be called **anthroposophy**.

Like the theosophical movement, Steiner's anthroposophy was a combination of elements from different philosophies and religions: Egyptian religious thought, *Buddhism*, Christian *gnosticism*, mystic literature, and classic German philosophy. The emphasis of this new movement was to connect the spirituality in people with the spiritual nature of the universe; the stumbling block that was preventing this from happening was materialism.

Steiner believed and wrote that thousands of years ago, humans had had much more of an understanding of, and influence upon, the spiritual world. Then the trap of materialism had shown itself, and humans had become less and less responsive to spiritual motivation; instead, they had succumbed to the mind-numbing power of material objects. The solution to this was to educate young people in a way that "grew" their spiritual selves.

Johann Wolfgang von Goethe

In 1913, Steiner established a headquarters for his movement, directing the construction of the Goetheaneum, a school building, in Dornach, Switzerland. Steiner's movement grew and became an educational system as well, leading to the formation of the Rudolf Steiner schools; the first school was founded in Stuttgart, Germany in 1919, for workers at the Waldorf-Astoria cigarette factory. The curriculum in these schools emphasizes creativity as a way of reaching spiritual insight. Today, thousands of young people around the world attend these institutions called **Waldorf schools**.

79. Vivekananda
(1863–1902)

Vivekananda

In the late 19th century, a member of India's upper-class caste system helped spread the revival of modern **Hinduism** begun by **Ramakrishna** (see no. 76).

Vivekananda was born **Narendranath Datta** in Calcutta, India in 1863. He was of the *kayastha* caste, the upper class in Indian society. Datta had a Western-style education and graduated from college. After his father's death, he became a follower of the religious leader Ramakrishna, a priest who led a revival of Hinduism through worship of Kali, the Hindu goddess.

From his guru Ramakrsihna, Datta adopted the belief that all religions pointed toward the same end-point, the same God, even though they took different routes. After Ramakrishna's death, Datta —who took the religious name Vivekananda—added aspects of his own thought. He came to believe that the Divine (God) presence has two distinct levels. The higher level cannot be known; in fact it cannot even be described, for it is without specific qualities. However, at the lower level it can be known; it has qualities and takes on forms, such as Kali, Christ, Buddha, or even Ramakrishna.

In 1893, Vivekananda left India for the first time. He went to the United States and addressed the World Parliament of Religions in Chicago. He made a powerful impression at the conference; while Hinduism was an ancient Indian religion, here was a new leader suggesting that all religions could work together on a positive path where all the various doctrines and myths would lead to the One.

In 1897, Vivekananda returned to India a famous man. Inspired by his travels, he founded the **Ramakrishna Mission** in Calcutta; its goal was to teach social reform, perform works of education and social service, and preach a universal Hinduism.

Vivekananda called for all religions to embrace his concept of One World through the integration of science and sacred literature (*Veda*). Hinduism had an advantage over Christianity in this respect. The latter was trying to sort out the meaning and implication of Charles Darwin's study of evolution, while the ancient Hindu texts had always spoken of something akin to evolution. This was one reason why many Indians accepted the caste system—they believed that all would be put right in the future.

Vivkenanda died in 1902 at the age of 39. In his short lifetime, he had brought a new vitality to Hinduism, and presented that faith to other parts of the world. He had also given many Indians a new pride in their heritage.

80. Mohandas Gandhi
(1869–1948)

One of the most remarkable leaders of the 20th century, **Mohandas Gandhi** combined spirituality with political skills to free his people and change the course of history.

Mohandas Karamchand Gandhi was born in the seaport city of Porbandar, India in 1869. As a youth, he was influenced by Muslim friends and Hindu family members. He also became an adherent of **Jainism**—the doctrine of noninjury to all living things—which would eventually lead to his belief in the use of nonviolence in the pursuit of social justice.

Gandhi sailed for London in 1887 to study the law. He returned to India in 1889; in 1893, he went to **South Africa** to become a law clerk. Gandhi and his fellow Indians were treated as lower class people in South Africa. Gandhi became determined to get just treatment for his people. During the next 10 years, he formulated his concept of *satyagraha*. Although **Henry David Thoreau's** ideas of civil disobedience were his starting point, Gandhi went well beyond that notion. *Satyagraha* meant "grasping or holding to truth," and a true practitioner would do so regardless of the consequences, including death.

Gandhi returned to India in 1915. At the time, Great Britain ruled over hundreds of millions of Indians, who were divided amongst themselves because of the caste system. Gandhi announced a movement intended to bring an end to British rule. He gave up his suit and tie for the simple clothes of the "untouchables," India's lowest social class. He spun fabric on his spinning wheel every day, and urged his fellows to do the same. He also conducted a number of fasts, each one designed to protest continuing British rule.

Given the name Mahatma, **"great soul,"** Gandhi soon became the spiritual leader of a

Mohandas Gandhi

movement that was to attract millions of supporters to the cause of **Indian independence**. While he firmly advocated **nonviolent protest**, he also promoted the idea of noncooperation with British rulers, a stance that led to his arrest on numerous occasions. Gandhi was also deeply concerned about the rift between Hindus and Muslims in India; he tried to bring the two groups together in a common struggle to persuade the British to leave India.

Gandhi's peaceful revolution succeeded; the British left India in 1947. However, for Gandhi the victory was marred by the fact that India was partitioned; the Hindu-dominant region became India, while the Muslim-dominant region became Pakistan.

While Gandhi lived to see his dream of an independent India realized, the continuing Hindu-Muslim hatred brought tragedy. On January 30, 1948, he was assassinated by a *Hindu* fanatic who believed that Gandhi had developed too much sympathy for the Muslim cause.

81. Albert Schweitzer
(1875–1965)

Physician, theologian, musician, and humanitarian, **Albert Schweitzer** was one of the most inspiring people of the 20th century.

The son of a *Protestant* minister, Albert Schweitzer was born in Kayersberg, Alsace in 1875. Just five years earlier, that province had been taken from France by Germany, and Schweitzer grew up in a land that had a mixed Franco-German heritage.

As a young man, Schweitzer displayed amazing intellectual prowess. By the age of 30 he had earned two doctorates: one in music and another in theology. His book, *J.S. Bach* (1905), remained the standard biography of the great composer for many years. In addition Schweitzer played the organ so well that he could earn a handsome living just by giving occasional concerts.

Albert Schweitzer

Schweitzer became equally famous for his theological works. In books such as *The Mystery of the Kingdom of God* (1901), and *The Quest of the Historical Jesus* (1906), Schweitzer explored the teachings of Jesus in detail, and presented the theory that when seen in historical perspective, Jesus is a enigma to the modern mind. Throughout these early years, the royalties Schweitzer earned from his books on Bach and Christ allowed him to live comfortably.

At the age of 30, Schweitzer chose to give up this life of scholarship and music, and devote the rest of his life to humanitarian service. He studied medicine in Strasbourg, and in 1913, he and his wife, **Helene Bresslau**, a trained nurse, left Europe. They settled in the village of Lambaréné, on the Ogowe River in what was then **French Equatorial Africa** (present-day Republic of Gabon). There they built a hospital and began to treat Africans for dysentery, malaria, and many other diseases.

World War I interrupted their mission and the Schweitzers were forced to return to Europe for a time. When they returned to the jungle in 1924, Schweitzer found his original hospital in ruins. Undeterred, he began to rebuild, and was soon treating more people than ever. They came on foot and by dugout canoe to see the "Grand Docteur" who had devoted his life to serving them.

Visitors began to come from other countries. Journalists began to visit the settlement and hospital built in the jungle where Schweitzer demonstrated by example the phrase he made famous: **"reverence for life."** Before long, he became known throughout the world, and **Lambaréné** became the best-known hospital in Africa.

During the 1950s, Schweitzer became an outspoken opponent of the spread of nuclear arms. He made many speeches urging the United States and the Soviet Union to stop the growing arms race and give up atomic weapons.

In recognition for his lifetime of humanitarian work, Albert Schweitzer was awarded the **Nobel Peace Prize** in 1952.

Some people called him the "Sleeping Prophet." Others considered him delusional. However, of the many people who met **Edgar Cayce**, very few doubted his sincerity. He believed that he was channeling spirit energy, and those who believed him became practically his disciples.

Cayce was born near Hopkinsville, Kentucky in 1877. He left school as an adolescent and became an apprentice to a photographer. In 1903, he married **Gertrude Evans**, and the couple eventually had three sons.

Cayce claimed that he healed himself of chronic laryngitis by going into a trance state, diagnosing himself, and prescribing both hypnotic and herbal remedies for the condition. Soon afterward, he found that neighbors and friends wished to be healed of their ailments, so he began to diagnose and prescribe for them—often with positive results. During these early years, he remained very much a homespun healer; he had never learned to read, so people were taken by his simple manner. Then, on October 9, 1910, the *New York Times* ran an article titled "Illiterate Man Becomes a Doctor When Hypnotized." From then on, thousands of people came to his door, some of them traveling from a great distance.

Cayce found that he needed to systematize his trance states and healing prescriptions. Therefore, each time he went into a trance, his wife, who controlled the questioning, was present. There was also a secretary who took careful minutes of each session.

"We see the body," or "We have the body" is how Cayce began most of his psychic readings. A new element was added in 1923, when Cayce was befriended by **Arthur Lammers**, a wealthy student of Eastern religions. Cayce soon added the words and concepts of *karma*, *reincarnation*, and **past lives** to his readings. He dwelt at length on the existence of Atlantis, and the coming earth changes that he believed would dramatically alter society in the future.

Morton Blumenthal, a New York City stockbroker, was the second of Cayce's patrons. Blumenthal funded the creation of the Cayce Hospital and the Atlantic University in Virginia Beach, but both enterprises failed in 1931 as the Great Depression took hold. Cayce's family and friends then founded the **Association for Research and Enlightenment** at Virginia Beach, and he continued with his work for the remainder of his life.

By the 1960s, Cayce was called **"America's best known psychic."** At the time of his death, he had performed more than 14,000 readings, all of which are available at the Edgar Cayce Foundation in Virginia Beach, Virginia.

Edgar Cayce

Edgar Cayce's psychic readings provide an important link between the folk healing tradition of the Appalachian Mountain areas and the "New Age" beliefs of the 1980s and 1990s.

83. Martin Buber
(1878–1965)

Philosopher and theologian, **Martin Buber** explored **Jewish mysticism** and the nature of human beings' interpersonal relationships with other humans, as well as their relationship to God.

Buber was born in Vienna, the capital of the Austro-Hungarian Empire, in 1878. His mother abandoned her husband and child when Buber was four, and he was raised for a number of years by his paternal grandparents. His grandfather Salomon Buber was one of the last great scholars of the *Haskalah*, the Jewish Enlightenment that had flourished in the wake of Moses Mendelssohn (see no. 68).

Buber was educated in the best traditions of both Judaic learning and secular 19th century studies. He married **Paula Winkler**, a Catholic, and she gave up her religion and her family of origin to devote herself to him. Her encouragement and assistance helped give Buber the strength to examine **Hasidism**, a Jewish mysticism that had flourished in Poland during the 18th century.

Traditional Jewish scholars had always stayed away from Hasidism, perceiving it as a form of the occult. Buber changed that; during the course of more than 30 years study and writing, he brought about a new point of view: that Hasidism was one of the great mystical traditions of the world, and that Jews should be proud of it.

Buber believed that God was imminent and present in every moment. He believed that many people miss their experience of God because they approach religion as they do life, from the perspective of "I-It." This means that life is a thing, an "it" which is to be experienced, and as such it remains forever distant.

What Buber called for instead was an "I-Thou" approach—to other people, to life, and to God. In the "I-Thou," people relate to others as they truly are, seeing them as ends in themselves. In this realm, the presence of God is revealed. Buber believed that life is an endless dialogue with God, one that does not endanger peoples' freedom or creativity. Buber's philosophy broke with Jewish tradition; he did not believe in the concept of God as a lawgiver, consequently he held no special regard for the **Torah**. This is one reason why over the years his beliefs became more **popular with Christians** than with Jews.

Buber published his beliefs in *Ich und du* in 1922; it was later translated to English and published as *I and Thou* in 1937. Buber and his family moved to Palestine in 1938, and he became an advocate for a joint Arab-Jewish state. This contributed to his unpopularity at times with his fellow Jews; however, during his lifetime Buber's views had reached a wide audience—that of humane and learned people throughout the world.

Martin Buber

84. Angelo Roncalli (Pope John XXIII)
(1881–1963)

When he became pope in 1958, people expected him to be a conscientious but dull leader. However, they had not studied the man; Pope **John XXIII** became the most active and beloved of 20th century pontiffs.

Angelo Giuseppe Roncalli was born in the tiny hamlet of Sotto il Monte, in the foothills of the Italian Alps. The first boy in a family of 13 children, he underwent his religious training at the seminary of Bergamo, then went on to Rome. He was *ordained* in 1904.

Roncalli served as a sergeant in the Italian medical corps during **World War I**. This experience broadened his view of life; he would be one of the few popes who had witnessed human suffering on a large scale and in a first-hand manner.

Raised to archbishop in 1925, Roncalli was sent on a number of prestigious diplomatic assignments. He spent nearly 20 years in the eastern Mediterranean, and during World War II, he played an important role in rescuing Jews in Hungary, Bulgaria, and Turkey. In 1945, he became the pope's representative to the newly liberated France. Roncalli became a cardinal in 1953, and served as patriarch of Venice. Despite his stature within the Church, many people were surprised when he was elected pope on October 28, 1958, at the age of 76. People were even more surprised when he took the name John XXIII; the name John had been out of favor for centuries.

As pope, John XXIII became a leader in the new **ecumenical movement** that was gaining strength around the world. He received the leading members of many other faiths, including the Archbishop of Canterbury. Whether Catholic or *Protestant*, Jewish or *agnostic*, nearly all those who met him were entranced by the pope's humor, gentle manner, and kindly disposition.

The pope surprised even his own coun-selors when he called for a **Second Vatican Council**. A gathering of nearly 3,000 of the world's Catholic bishops, as well as lay Catholics, the council convened on October 11, 1962. Although he did not attend the council's sessions, the pope's influence was felt by the participants. The council would eventually reorient the Church's teachings on such various issues as modern technology, education, war and peace, *atheism*, the Jewish people, and the education of the clergy.

Pope John XXIII

John XXIII was very concerned with the plight of the world's poor people, and his papal encyclicals urged nations to defend human rights. The pope was also instrumental in doing much to erase anti-Semitism within the Catholic church.

Pope John XXIII died in June 1963. His brief five-year papacy had brought a new, more enlightened and vigorous style to the Catholic church.

91

85. Kahlil Gibran
(1883–1931)

Kahil Gibran

Kahlil Gibran's mystical writing style moved a generation of spiritual seekers, and his finest work, *The Prophet*, remains one of the most popular spiritual works ever published.

Gibran was born in Besharri, Lebanon, in 1883. At the time part of the Ottoman Empire, Besharri was a small village beneath Mount Lebanon, inhabited largely by Maronite Christians. Gibran grew up in an atmosphere rich with cultural and religious diversity; Syrians, Lebanese, Palestinians, and Turks all passed through the region, as did members of all the major religions.

Gibran, however, did not enjoy a happy childhood. His father was a gambler, and after he was prosecuted for embezzlement, Gibran's mother took her four children and boarded a ship for the United States. In 1895, the family settled in South Boston, Massachusetts, where his mother opened a dry goods store.

The teenage Gibran's artistic skill was noticed by a settlement-house teacher. One contact led to another, and Gibran enjoyed the financial and moral support of two important patrons: Fred Holland Day and Mary Elizabeth Haskell. Because of their help, he was able to study art in Paris.

Tragedy struck in 1902. Gibran's mother, his sister, and his half-brother all died within the space of a year. Devastated by the losses, he withdrew more into his art and poetry. It was probably then that he formed the kernel of what became his spiritual hallmark: acceptance and love of whatever is given by God.

By 1915, Gibran was living in New York City, where he enjoyed a wide array of friends and admirers. He was hard at work on what became his masterpiece, *The Prophet*, published in October 1923. It sold a thousand copies in the first month; soon, mostly through word-of-mouth recommendation, it became hugely popular. Over the many years it has been in print, it has gone on to sell more than eight million copies.

In *The Prophet*, the crowd asks the holy man to, "Speak to us of Knowledge," or "Speak to us of Marriage," or whatever other major concerns they have. To all, the holy man responds with answers of **liberation, release**, and **acceptance**. He urges people to run naked in the rain, to love whom and when they can, and not to be constrained by the need for social acceptance. Yet *The Prophet* is not an anarchistic book; Gibran's solemn tones remind the reader that life is full of turmoil and tragedy from which no one escapes. The point is to live fully, and to embrace whatever gifts the Universe provides.

Gibran died in New York City in 1931. With his brilliant spiritual work, he left behind a rich legacy that still delights and haunts readers throughout the world today.

A German born theologian and philosopher spent his life's work addressing the implications of *existentialism* for Christianity and exploring the relationship between theology and culture.

Paul Johannes Tillich was born in Starzeddel, East Prussia in 1886, the son of a Lutheran pastor. The family moved to Berlin, Germany in 1900, and Tillich went on to study theology at several German universities. He was ordained as a Lutheran minister in 1912.

In 1914, Tillich volunteered to serve as a chaplain in the Prussian-German army during **World War I**. The war provided a severe trial by fire for Tillich. He drew comfort and strength from the good-heartedness he observed among the common soldiers, but grew more and more discontented with his church which had lent its support to the war in the first place.

After Tillich's service ended in 1918, he became a lecturer in theology at Berlin University. In the 1920s, he taught theology and philosophy at various universities; in 1929, he became chairman of the philosophy department at the University of Frankfurt.

During the 1920s, Tillich began to publish writings **examining religion and culture**, as well as Christianity's role in civilization in relation to the new philosophy of existentialism. Tillich believed that it was important for theologians to connect in some meaningful way the foundation of Christianity with the questions raised by the existentialist view of being and nonbeing. Tillich considered God as the "Ground of being" and human existence as part of God.

In 1933, Tillich was dismissed from his position at Frankfurt for his opposition to the new Nazi regime. He immigrated to the United States, and began to teach at both Union Theological Seminary and Columbia University, in New York City. Tillich became an American citizen in 1940 and a minister of the Evangelical and Reformed Church.

Tillich's greatest impact came through his writings. He published *The Courage to Be* in 1952; it became an immediate sensation in theological schools and seminaries across the United States. His most comprehensive work, *Systematic Theology*, was published in three volumes between 1951 and 1963.

Tillich was not a comforting theologian. He believed that the concept of an all-powerful God—one who involved himself with the workings of the universe—was nonsense; instead, he believed strongly in human freedom and creativity. He felt that God should not be viewed as a personal God, "a Being" superior to humans, but as some higher concept.

Tillich's name and fame grew as the existential philosophy gained more adherents in the United States and Europe. An entire generation of *Protestant* pastors read his works, and many of them became **social activists** during the 1960s.

Paul Tillich

He never wore a collar and he never preached a sermon. Just the same, **Bill Wilson** was one of the important American spiritual leaders of the 20th century.

Wilson was born in East Dorset, Vermont in 1895. His early life was anything but secure. Wilson's father deserted the family when the boy was 10, and his mother left for Boston where she pursued a new career as an osteopathic physician. The boy and his sister were left in the care of their maternal grandparents.

Bill Wilson

Wilson enlisted for service in **World War I**. During his training period, he took his first alcoholic drink, and was soon hooked. The feeling of abandonment by his parents had clung to him, and he found that alcohol provided a major release for his insecurities.

Neither success as a soldier, nor his marriage to **Lois Burnham** improved his self-esteem. During the 1920s, the young couple speculated in stock investments and did reasonably well. Then the bottom fell out when the stock market crashed in 1929. Wilson's **alcoholism** steadily worsened.

On a cold, dank day in November 1934, Wilson offered one of his steady drinking buddies a drink. The friend declined. "No, I don't need it," the friend replied. "I've got religion."

Dumbfounded, Wilson sought out what his friend had found. Wilson experienced a spiritual awakening sometime that winter, and on June 10, 1935, he and **Dr. Robert Smith**, an Akron, Ohio surgeon, founded **Alcoholics Anonymous**. (The men were known as Bill W. and Dr. Bob S. to reinforce the group's desire to respect an alcoholic's anonymity.) What they had discovered was that alcoholism was a disease, and that the fellowship and company of other alcoholics was essential for their own recovery.

In 1939, the group published its basic textbook, *Alcoholics Anonymous*, written by Bill W. The book explained A.A.'s philosophy and methods, with the heart of the suggested program being contained in the **Twelve Steps** of recovery.

The basis of the Twelve Step program was for a person to acknowledge: an addiction to alcohol; a need for God to help him overcome the addiction; that because of the addiction, persons have been harmed, and amends needed to be made; and, having had a spiritual awakening as a result of these steps, the message should be carried to other alcoholics.

By the time Bill Wilson died in 1971, there were more than one million participants in the program. By the end of the 20th century, there were more than 50,000 separate Alcoholics Anonymous groups within the United States, as well as thousands of groups in Canada, and around the world. In addition, the Twelve Step AA program has become the premise of many other groups, including **Overeaters Anonymous** and **Gamblers Anonymous**.

Socialist, journalist, and convert to Catholicism, **Dorothy Day** devoted her life to issues of social justice and international peace.

Day was born in Brooklyn, New York in 1897; her family later moved to Oakland, California, and then to Chicago. As a young woman, Day was an active member of the **American Socialist Party** and she protested against American involvement in World War I.

For a time after the war, Day led a bohemian life in Greenwich Village. She had several disastrous romantic relationships, including a one-year marriage. In her early 20s, Day had an abortion, and thereafter suffered both guilt and fear that she would never be a mother. In the mid-1920s, she settled in Staten Island, New York as the common-law wife of **Firster Batterham**, a fisherman and anarchist. She was overjoyed when she gave birth to Tamar, her one and only child, in March 1926. Though she still was an *agnostic*, Day had her daughter baptized in the Catholic church, as a sign of thanksgiving for the birth. After more than a year of soul searching, Day herself was baptized a **Catholic** in December 1927.

From that time on she was a changed person. Where she previously had been bitter, confused, and even anarchistic, she now emerged as a beacon of light, faith, and hope.

The onset of the **Great Depression** during the 1930s brought forth a great need for people with Day's religious and social commitment. On May 1, 1933, she founded *The Catholic Worker*, a monthly newspaper, published in New York City. The paper drew heavily upon papal encyclicals on social justice, and its articles did much to relieve the distress of working-class Americans. Day also started soup kitchens in New York, and helped co-found *Homes of Hospitality*, for the homeless and the elderly in need. Throughout this period, Day ministered to the sick, fed

the poor, and spread the Catholic gospel. She soon became the most influential Catholic lay person in the United States.

All of Day's good work was nearly undone during World War II. A **committed pacifist**, she urged complete noncooperation with the U.S. Selective Service and the draft, and her popularity fell dramatically during the 1940s. Only the threat of nuclear war, heightened by the destruction of Hiroshima and Nagasaki, brought some measure of balance to Day's reputation.

Dorothy Day

Day became more conservative as she grew older, and she was somewhat out of step with the liberation movements of the 1960s (Thirty years earlier she would probably have led them!) She died in 1980, after a richly textured life in which she had progressed through radicalism, the fight for social justice, conversion to Catholicism, and the alteration of American perceptions of that faith.

89. C.S. Lewis
(1898–1963)

English literary scholar, novelist, and popular theologian, **C.S. Lewis** spread his vision of spirituality and Christianity to millions of readers—young and old—during his lifetime.

Clive Staples Lewis was born in Belfast, Ireland in 1898. He served in World War I, and graduated from University College at Oxford in 1923. From then on, he was a university fellow, either at Oxford or at Cambridge, and he won high distinction for his **literary scholarship** in such fields as classic and Renaissance literature.

C.S. Lewis, on the cover of *Time* magazine

While Lewis achieved great academic success, by the 1940s, his writings began to bring him much popular acclaim. After an early period of *rationalism*, Lewis became a convinced Christian, and began to devote his writings to the subject of **Christian ethics**. His first major work in this area was *The Problem of Pain*, published in 1940. In an era when many spiritual teachers offered "easy grace," Lewis pointed to the value of spiritual and physical pain. Only pain, he wrote, makes us fully human, and leads us to embrace our need for God.

Then came *The Screwtape Letters* (1942), considered by many to be Lewis's masterpiece. This short book is deceptive; it appears easy to read, but it draws the reader into an awareness of the many ways he can fall short of truly Christian attitudes. It points to the many habits which humans have that allow the dark forces (the Devil and his angels) to seduce them. Lewis pointed to the ambiguity in the word "spiritual." "There is spiritual evil as well as spiritual good...the worst sins of men are spiritual."

During the 1950s, Lewis displayed his literary versatility by creating a brilliant series of fiction for young people. The seven *Chronicles of Narnia* (1950-1956), include such classics as *The Horse and His Boy*, and *The Lion, The Witch, and the Wardrobe*. As with his writings for adults, these books concern not only moral choices, but spiritual presences and the eternal reality behind appearances.

When he was well into his fifties, the unmarried Lewis met and fell in love with an American woman named **Helen Joy**. They married in 1956, and while she provided the personal, one-to-one love he had desired all his life, their happiness was short-lived. She died in 1960; Lewis expressed his distress over her death in his book *A Grief Observed* (1961).

Throughout his life, C.S. Lewis had divided his career between the academic world of English scholarship and the literary world where he considered the moral, ethical, and religious questions confronting humanity in the 20th century. By the time of his death in 1963, he was one of the most beloved and respected of all Christian authors.

90. Ruhollah Hendi (Ayatollah Khomeini) (1900–1989)

Americans remember him as one of their most villainous enemies. Islamic Iranians recall him as the greatest spiritual leader of the 20th century.

Ruhollah Hendi was born in the small town of Khomein on the edge of the desert in west-central Persia (present-day Iran). Later he dropped his family name and adopted the name of his native village.

The son and grandson of religious leaders, Khomeini studied traditional Islamic theology in Qom, an ancient city about 100 miles south of Teheran. He became a revered teacher of religion, and wrote many works on Islamic philosophy, law and ethics; as he devoted his life to Islamic studies, he began to be called **ayatollah**, a title of religious distinction.

Beginning in 1941, **Muhammad Reza Pahlavi** became the ruler—or shah—of Iran. Supported by the West, and particularly the United States, Pahlavi wanted to create a modern, western-style technocratic state, and he had considerable success. However, the shah ran into a form of **spiritual resistance**, led by Khomeini, that proved to be irresistible.

By the early 1960s, Khomeini began to criticize the shah and his policies, which, Khomeini asserted, constituted an adulteration of Islam. Khomeini was **exiled** from Iran in 1964. He lived for many years in Iraq, but was then expelled from that country as well. In October 1978, he settled outside Paris.

Over the next year, Khomeini worked hard from France to overthrow the shah, secretly sending taped messages to faithful groups within Iran. **A popular revolution** broke out, and the shah went into exile on January 16, 1979; Khomeini returned in triumph on January 30. While he took no official title, and he lived in Qom, rather than the political capital of Teheran, it was evident that Khomeini was Iran's ruler. He had succeeded in creating a true *theocracy*.

Khomeini established revolutionary tribunals that conducted summary trials of Iranians who had supported the shah; many defendants were found guilty and executed. Khomeini completely infuriated the West when he condoned the seizure of the U.S. embassy in Teheran by Iranian students on November 4, 1979. The students took 53 Americans hostage, beginning an ordeal that would last for 444 days. Night after night, Americans witnessed Iranians chanting "The Great Satan," and "Death to America" on the nightly news, while Americans held their own anti-Iranian demonstrations.

Ayatollah Khomeini

U.S. President **Jimmy Carter** was powerless in the situation. Carter became unpopular at home, and lost the 1980 presidential election to Ronald Reagan. On Reagan's inauguration day, January 20, 1981, Iran freed the hostages.

Khomeini ruled Iran until his death in 1989. Hated in the West, he was revered in Iran as the spiritual leader who brought Islam back to his country.

"To be able to love the poor and know the poor, we must be poor ourselves." **Mother Teresa** followed this belief her entire life, and she was a shining example of the difference that one human being can make in a world full of suffering.

Agnes Gonxha Bojaxhiu was born to Albanian parents in Skopje, Macedonia in 1910. Her father was a grocer; prior to that, the family had been farmers for many generations.

Mother Teresa

When she was 17 years-old, Agnes traveled to Ireland to join the order of the sisters of **Our Lady of Loreto**. She learned to speak English, took the name Sister Teresa, and was trained in the religious life. By the time she took her final vows in 1937, she was in **Calcutta**, India, teaching at a convent school, where she became the headmistress. She spent a number of years teaching happily, but in 1946 she received what she described as a "call within a call." She came to believe that her new mission was to **minister to the poorest of the poor**, of whom there were thousands, if not millions, in Calcutta.

From that time forward, Teresa dressed in a sari and went barefoot through the city slums. In 1950, she became an Indian citizen, and also received approval from the Vatican for her new **Order of the Missionaries of Charity**. One of the most important of the Order's requirements was a strict vow of poverty; none of the brothers or sisters was to own private property.

At first she and about a dozen followers conducted their work in anonymity. However, during the late 1960s, television documentaries in England and the United States showcased the remarkable woman working in Calcutta. Her face became known to millions of people around the world. Before long, she was traveling to other countries to help the poor, rescue children, and advise other groups providing assistance to the less fortunate.

Mother Teresa was a ball of quiet energy. Of small and slight stature, she nonetheless radiated a spiritual energy and calmness that touched nearly everyone she met. Some people questioned whether her work made enough of a difference, in a world so full of hungry and desperate people. Mother Teresa herself never thought of her work in statistical terms; as she put it, how can one measure the value of a person's happiness or well being, even if it is temporary?

In 1979, Mother Teresa's tireless efforts in behalf of the poor were recognized when she was awarded the **Nobel Peace Prize**. When she died on September 5, 1997, people around the world mourned the passing of one of the 20th century's greatest humanitarians.

Many people revere him for his insight and direction, while others denounce him as a fraud. On balance, there is no doubt that **L.R. Hubbard** influenced millions of people, and brought forth a new type of spiritual "cleansing."

Lafayette Ronald Hubbard was born in Tilden, Nebraska in 1911. His father served in the U.S. Navy, and Lafayette spent much of his youth with his maternal grandparents in Montana. Early on, Lafayette developed a wanderlust, and by the time he entered George Washington University in 1930 he had already visited a number of Pacific islands.

Beginning around 1934, Hubbard made a career for himself as a **science fiction writer**. Using a number of different pen names, he employed his tremendous imagination to a variety of topics, and became one of the most prolific science fiction authors of the time.

Up until 1950, there was nothing in his life to predict his emergence as a spiritual leader. However, in that year, under the name L. Ron Hubbard, he published *Dianetics: The Modern Science of Mental Health*. In the book, Hubbard described his theory that every person's mind has two distinct sections: the **analytical mind** and the **reactive mind**. Within the reactive mind are stored "engrams," which encompass such things as fear, suspicion, superstition, and paranoia. According to Hubbard, everyone wants to be freed from their "engrams," but the only way to do so is to work with a counselor (or "auditor") trained in the methods of Dianetics.

The book was a smashing success. As a result, in 1953, Hubbard founded the **Church of Scientology**. He moved to England in 1959, and supervised the education of many auditors. The Hubbard Association of Scientologists International grew rapidly, and Hubbard soon became a household name in Europe, as well as the United States.

L. Ron Hubbard

However, the movement was not without controversy. In 1968, British authorities refused to allow Scientology students and teachers to enter the country on the grounds that Scientology was "**socially harmful**," and that its authoritarian principles posed a danger to those who would be followers.

In the late 1960s, Hubbard resigned all his posts within the Church of Scientology. He recruited and trained a small number of willing adherents, and announced the creation of a "**Sea Organization**," meant to travel the oceans of the world while refining the concepts of Scientology. In 1967, Hubbard boarded his large yacht, the *Royal Scotman*, and spent the next several years cruising the world.

Hubbard returned to land in 1976, and moved to a desert ranch in La Quinta, California. He died in Creston, California in 1986. After his death, Scientology continued to be one of the most popular—and controversial—movements of the late 20th century.

Thomas Merton

A Trappist monk who found **Catholicism** after of years of spiritual wandering helped change the lives of countless spiritual seekers during the 1950s and 60s.

Thomas Merton was born in Prades, France in 1915. His family moved to the United States the following year. Merton's American mother died when he was six; his father, a native of New Zealand, died when Merton was 16.

After studying for a year at Clare College in Cambridge, England, Merton returned to the United States and earned his masters in English at Columbia University. Life as an orphan combined with a powerful intellect to make Merton a wanderer and experimenter; as a young man, he took up a lifestyle of drugs, promiscuous sexual relationships, and other aspects of Bohemian living. Then in 1938 he found the Catholic church, and his life took a dramatic turn in another direction.

After teaching for two years at St. Bonaventure University, Merton entered the monastery of Gethsemani of the **Cistercians of the Strict Observance** in Bardstown, Kentucky in December, 1941. Popularly known as "Trappists," the Cistercian monks purposely seclude themselves from the world and its distractions. Merton entered wholly into this lifestyle, but he also accepted the encouragement of his superiors to write.

Write he did. In 1948, Merton's spiritual autobiography, *The Seven Storey Mountain*, was published. It became a best-seller, largely through word of mouth. The book tells the story of Merton's spiritual confusions early in his life, and his conversion to Catholicism. For decades after, countless people—scholars, priests, and spiritual seekers—would publicly announce that reading *The Seven Storey Mountain* had been a landmark event in their lives.

During the tumultuous 1960s, Merton paid more attention to "outer" worldly events. His *hermitage* at the *monastery* became something of a pilgrimage stop for idealists and activists. In 1968, he asked his superiors for permission to travel to Thailand for a major convention of Buddhist monks. This was unprecedented; a Trappist monk took a lifetime vow of retreat from the outside world. However, the *abbot* gave his permission, and late in the year Merton went to India.

On November 4, 1968, Merton met the Dalai Lama (see no. 100) at Dharmasala. The two men found a common spiritual ground. When they parted, the Lama praised Merton as someone of high learning. Merton then went on to Bangkok, where he gave the opening address to the Buddhist monks' convention.

Tragically, a few hours later, Merton was found dead in his hotel room after being electrocuted in his bathtub. The date was December 10, 1968, 27 years to the day since he had entered the monastery of Gethsemani, where his body was taken for burial.

94. Alan Watts
(1915–1973)

Prolific author, teacher, and lecturer, **Alan Watts** was one of the most prominent interpreters of **Eastern religions** and philosophies for the West for more than 40 years.

Alan Wilson Watts was born in Chiselhurst, England in 1915. His interest in Eastern religions grew out of his fascination with Indian and Chinese art. An excellent student, he began his religious reading at an early age. When he was 16, he wrote essays for the Buddhist Lodge in London, and he published his first book, *The Spirit of Zen*, when he was only 20 years-old.

Watts was far ahead of his time; among the British youth he had grown up with, it was fashionable to downplay any real significance in Eastern spirituality. That of course would change as the horrors of World War II exposed the British, and Europeans in general, to the weaknesses inherent in their own cultural beliefs and customs.

Watts married an American woman in 1938, and the couple moved to Long Island, New York. He then studied for the **Episcopalian priesthood** and was *ordained* in 1944.

The year 1950 was a crucial one for Watts. His marriage ended; he married again, and he left both the priesthood and the Episcopal Church. When people questioned him about the roots of his own beliefs, Watts would respond, "I do not label myself a Zen Buddhist, nor belong to any religious sect, on the ground that partisanship in religion closes the mind." He taught comparative philosophy and psychology for a few years, and then became a full-time writer and lecturer.

During the 1950s, Watts's personal theology evolved. At the deepest level of being, Watts believed that there was no separation and no duality; in other words, each and every person has a direct line of communication with the universe and whatever god or

Alan Watts

gods exist. By coming to full realization of this, anyone can experience the liberation and joy of being that follows from this way of thought.

Meanwhile, the books kept coming. Watts wrote *Behold the Spirit* (1947), *The Supreme Identity* (1950), *The Way of Zen* (1957), *Nature, Man, and Woman* (1958), *This Is It* (1960), *Psychotherapy East and West* (1961), and *The Book: On the Taboo Against Knowing Who You Are* (1966). All of his writings and lectures demonstrated a fluidity of thought that could entice and often persuade even the most skeptical readers and listeners.

As is often the case with profound spiritual leaders, Watts had a difficult and troubled personal life. He married three times, and had a total of seven children. During his later years, he drank heavily, which contributed to his death in 1973.

Oscar Romero
(1917–1980)

When he became Catholic archbishop of El Salvador in 1977, **Oscar Romero** expected, and was expected to be, a conservative leader. Just three years later, he had become the conscience of the Catholic church in his country and was on his way to **martyrdom** in the cause of liberation for oppressed people.

Oscar Romero was born at Ciudad Barrios, near the border with Honduras, in 1917. His father was a telegraph operator. As a boy, Romero was apprenticed to a carpenter, but in 1931 he enrolled in San Miguel Seminary. Romero was *ordained* a priest in 1942, and began to rise slowly through the Church ranks. He became an auxiliary bishop in 1970, bishop of Santiago de Maria in 1974, and in February 1977, was named **archbishop** of all El Salvador.

Until the mid-1970s, Oscar Romero had clung to a moderate, traditional interpretation of Catholic doctrine; he believed that the Church must minister to the needs of the poor and afflicted, but that it could not involve itself in political or social controversies. This was the standard belief of the Catholic hierarchy in Central and South America, although it was coming under attack from those priests who believed in what they called "**Liberation Theology**," which involved both uplifting and educating the poor. The movement was controversial both inside and outside the Church because it was anticapitalist and somewhat revolutionary in spirit.

By 1977, El Salvador was a troubled nation. Gunmen roamed the streets of many villages; people lived in various stages of poverty, and there was little hope for any improvement in their lives. Carlos Humberto Romero (no relation to Oscar Romero) seized control of the country in a coup in October 1979, making prospects for reform even dimmer.

By 1980, Archbishop Romero had become highly critical and outspoken in his condemnation of the various factions that were looking to control El Salvador and who at the same time were tearing the country apart—the dictator Carlos Romero, the military-civilian regime that deposed him, and the leftist guerrillas seeking to gain power.

There were repeated attempts on Archbishop Romero's life, but he refused to remain silent. In 1979, he had been nominated for the Nobel Peace Prize for his efforts on behalf of his county's poor people. Tragically, Romero's enemies finally caught up with him; he was **assassinated** as he celebrated Mass at the altar of the chapel in the Divine Providence Hospital in San Salvador in March 1980. Days later, his funeral Mass was broken up by the explosion of bombs and machine-gun fire.

Despite his violent death, Archbishop Romero had become the hero of those who believed in the cause of **social justice** and the Catholic church's active role in that cause.

Oscar Romero

96. Billy Graham
(1918–)

William Franklin Graham was born on a farm in Charlotte, North Carolina in 1918. On both sides of the family he was descended from Scottish-Irish pioneers, and both of his grandfathers had been Confederate soldiers during the Civil War.

Graham's parents were Reformed Presbyterians, but he was a joyous and mischievous youth, and not especially religious. That changed when he made his "decision for Christ" at the age of 16 during a revival meeting in Charlotte. From that point on, he dedicated his life to Christ.

Graham graduated from the Florida Bible Institute (now Trinity College), and was *ordained* a **Southern Baptist minister** in 1939. He then went north to attend Wheaton College in Illinois; there he met his future wife, Ruth McCue Bell. Both Wheaton College and his marriage in 1943 had the effect of broadening him; Graham developed a larger world view.

During the late 1940s, Graham became an evangelist with the "**Youth for Christ**" movement, and he preached at numerous rallies throughout the Midwest. In 1950, after a series of very successful evangelistic meetings in Los Angeles, Graham formed the **Billy Graham Evangelistic Association**. It was a turning point in his career.

Graham soon took his evangelism abroad, conducting a series of "crusades" for Christ throughout the world. Graham did extremely well overseas; in fact, he probably attracted more converts and witnessed more "decisions for Christ" in England than he did in the United States.

In addition to taking his message to Great Britain, over the next 40 years, Graham led revivals in eastern Europe, Asia, Africa, and the former Soviet Union. A persuasive and convincing preacher, Graham was estimated to have preached the word of Christ to more people than any other person in history.

As Graham's reputation grew over the years, people from around the world wrote touching letters to him, informing him of the impact of his ministry on their lives. In addition, he spread the word of Christ by authoring several books including, *Calling Youth to Christ* (1947), *America's Hour of Decision* (1951), *Peace with God* (1954), *Seven Deadly Sins* (1956), *World Aflame* (1965), and *Answers to Life's Problems* (1988).

Billy Graham with President Carter

During his career Graham became personally acquainted with many world leaders, and became the confidant of several American presidents, beginning with President Harry Truman, and including Presidents Eisenhower, Kennedy, Nixon, Carter, Bush, and Clinton. It was no exaggeration to say that Reverend Graham was the unofficial "**chaplain to the Presidents.**"

No scandal has ever tainted Billy Graham's life or ministry. Throughout his life, he remained an earnest preacher with millions of followers who would say he thoroughly deserved the recognition and fame he received.

Karol Wojtyla (Pope John Paul II)
(1920–)

Pope John Paul II

His courage and charisma are recognized around the world. Even critics of his policies admit that Pope **John Paul II** is one of the 20th century's most influential leaders.

Karol Wojtyla was born in Wadowice, Poland in 1920. His mother died when he was nine years-old, but the boy had an irrepressible joy and an infectious optimism about life. After his country was conquered by the Nazis in 1939, Wojtyla had to work in a stone quarry and a chemical factory during the German occupation. At the same time, he pursued his studies at an underground seminary, and in 1946 he was *ordained* a priest in the Roman Catholic church.

Years of study and then teaching followed. Pope John XXIII (see no. 84) noticed Wojtyla's contribution during the Second Vatican Council in 1962, and he rose to archbishop and then to cardinal. On October 16, 1978, he was elected pope, the **first Slavic** person ever to hold the position, and the first non-Italian in more than 450 years.

In June 1979, Pope John Paul II traveled to his native Poland. The Nazi evil had long since been destroyed, but John Paul turned his attention to another totalitarian menace: that of the Soviet Union. He affirmed his support for the new Polish labor union, **Solidarity**, and its leader, Lech Walesa. The pope's support went a long way toward helping Walesa and Solidarity establish themselves as a legitimate voice of opposition to the Soviet-backed Polish government, and eventually led to the union and Walesa's rise to power in the late 1980s.

During the 1980s, Pope John Paul II became probably the most traveled of all world leaders. He visited places in the world no previous pope had gone to, and he reached out to enormous crowds that gathered everywhere he went. It is estimated that he has probably been seen in the flesh by more people than any other human being in history.

John Paul survived an **attempted assassination** in 1981. During the rest of the decade, his prominence and popularity grew, and the collapse of Eastern European communism and the fall of the Berlin Wall were credited at least in part to his vigilant stance against communism.

During the 1990s, Pope John Paul II became more controversial in doctrinal matters. American Catholics were surprised when he took a hard line on matters such as birth control, and the continuance of the all-male priesthood. However, as the century and millennium ended, he was both the most recognizable and perhaps the most respected spiritual leader in the world.

98. Martin Luther King, Jr.
(1929–1968)

Spiritual leader and civil rights champion, the Reverend Dr. **Martin Luther King, Jr.** inspired millions of people around the world before his untimely death at the hands of an assassin in 1968.

Michael King, Jr. was born in Atlanta, Georgia in 1929. Both his father and grandfather were Baptist preachers. In 1934, his father changed both his own name and that of his five-year old son to "Martin Luther " King to honor the hero of the *Protestant* Reformation.

As a young man, King decided to follow his father and grandfather into the ministry. After graduating from Morehouse College in 1948, and Crozer Theological Seminary in 1951, King earned his doctorate at Boston University. While living in Boston, he met and married **Coretta Scott**, a native of Alabama. In 1953, the couple moved to Montgomery, Alabama, where King became pastor of a Baptist church.

In 1955, racial tensions in Montgomery were ignited when an African-American woman named **Rosa Parks** refused to give up her seat to a white person on a segregated city bus. The African-American community united behind her protest, and King led a successful boycott of the city bus system that lasted for more than a year. As a result of the action, the U.S. Supreme Court eventually declared the segregated system unconstitutional.

During his time in college and the seminary, King had become a firm believer in **nonviolent resistance** as the only means by which to end the segregation policies in the American South. In this regard, King had become influenced by the victories **Mohandas Gandhi** (see no. 80) had won in India during the 1930s and 1940s.

Soon after the Montgomery boycott victory, King founded the SCLC (Southern Christian Leadership Conference). Over the next few years, he led **boycotts** and **peace marches** throughout Alabama, and by 1963 he was the most respected African-American leader in the country. On August 28, 1963, he gave a momentous speech to 200,000 supporters in Washington D.C., which was later seen as the high point of the civil rights movement. A year later King was awarded the **Nobel Peace Prize** for his efforts in the fight for civil rights.

By 1967, King began leading marches that focused on problems engendered by poverty as well as racism; in addition, he had become an outspoken critic of U.S. involvement in the Vietnam War. In April 1968, he was in Memphis, Tennessee preparing to lead a march in support of striking sanitation workers. The night before the march, he was shot and killed as he walked along a motel balcony. Both the nation and the world mourned his loss; in 1983, the United States made his birthday a national holiday.

Martin Luther King, Jr.

99. Desmond Tutu
(1931–)

Like many other spiritual leaders, **Desmond Tutu** came a long way from humble beginnings. He was born in Klerksdorp, South Africa, in 1931, the son of members of the bantu-Tswana tribe. Tutu was baptized a Methodist, but the entire family later converted to Anglicanism.

Tutu was inspired to seek public service from an early age. He trained as a teacher, like his father, and taught in a high school for three years. He later resigned in protest against the racial discrimination practiced within the school system. Tutu was *ordained* an **Anglican priest** in 1961, and rose rapidly through the ranks of his faith.

June 16, 1976, black residents of the ghetto township of Soweto rose up in a fury of protest and violence against apartheid. It was the beginning of a storm that would engulf South Africa for the next 15 years.

In the late 1970s and early 1980s, Tutu played a leading role in the struggle to end apartheid. He began to travel abroad and urge the people of other countries to boycott South African goods. As a result, his passport was confiscated, and he was forced to remain in South Africa. Tutu called for peace and justice, always claiming that he would work to protect the rights of white South Africans once apartheid was ended.

Desmond Tutu (left) outside St. George's Church

Tutu received the **Nobel Peace Prize** in 1984. Two years later, he became **Archbishop of Cape Town**, the leader of the *Anglican church* in his country; he was the first black person to hold that position.

Because of the efforts of spiritual leaders like Tutu and of political leaders like **Nelson Mandela**, apartheid came to an end in 1994. Mandela became the first president of a new, desegregated South Africa. Tutu became a key member of the **Truth and Reconciliation Committee**, designed to examine the wrongs done under the name of apartheid. The committee announced that if people came forward and declared the things they had done under apartheid, they would not be imprisoned. This policy showed the willingness of men such as Mandela and Tutu to allow the wounds of apartheid to heal and bring white and black South Africa together.

Like Mohandas Gandhi and Martin Luther King, Jr. before him, Tutu found a powerful cause, one that burned within him and impelled him to greater heights. That cause was to fight the South African system of social segregation—called **apartheid**—that was keeping the white and black populations separate and allowing a system of painful inequality to exist.

Tutu became the dean of Johannesburg in 1975, the bishop of Lesotho in 1976, and in 1978, he became the first black secretary of the South African Council of Churches. On

Tenzin Gyatso, the Fourteenth Dalai Lama (1935–)

In an age of rampant materialism and personal cynicism, the **Dalai Lama** stands as one of the beacons of spiritual hope that sustains people of many faiths.

Tenzin Gyatso was born in the town of Takster, in the province of Amdo, in the northeast corner of Tibet in 1935. When he was a young boy, he was found by learned and pious *lamas* who had set forth from Tibet's capital in search of the *reincarnation* of the first Dalai Lama, who had governed Tibet in the 14th century. The various tests which they put the child through confirmed for them that he was indeed the reincarnated spirit of all the previous Dalai Lamas, including the 13th one, who died in 1933. Gyatso was brought to the 1,000-room Potola Palace in Tibet's capital, Lhasa, and became known as "His Holiness" at the age of five.

This idyllic, though lonely, condition ended in 1950 when Communist China invaded and conquered Tibet. China had claimed sovereignty over Tibet since about 1720, but the Tibetans managed to keep their freedom until the Communist takeover under Mao Tse-tung. For several years, the Dalai Lama tried to work with the Communists; he even flew to China and met with Chairman Mao. All his efforts proved to be in vain; the Chinese Communists believed religion to be a crutch that should be eliminated.

In 1959, the Chinese government began to attack the national and religious identity of Tibet. An uprising followed, and when Chinese forces suppressed the revolt, the Dalai Lama was forced to flee Lhasa. He and a few followers evaded the Chinese patrols and arrived in India, where they were given political sanctuary. They were soon joined by thousands of other Tibetan refugees, and they built a town called **Dharmasala** in India.

During the 1960s, the Dalai Lama began to travel throughout Europe and to the United States. While he called attention to atrocities committed against his people by the Chinese Communists, he also became known for his strong belief in **nonviolence** and loving-kindness. Over the years, the Dalai Lama continued to act as a spokesperson for the plight of his country, and has written extensively on *Buddhism* and his search for **world peace**.

In 1989, the Dalai Lama was awarded the **Nobel Peace Prize** in recognition of his campaign for the nonviolent liberation of his homeland from Chinese rule. By the turn of the 21st century, he was widely admired for his gentleness and compassion, and had become one of the most recognizable spiritual leaders in the world.

The Fourteenth Dalai Lama

GLOSSARY

abbey a place of residence occupied by a community of persons living in religious seclusion; a monastery or a convent

abbot a man who is the superior of an abbey

absolution the forgiveness and release of an individual from his or her sins; Catholics believe it has to be formally given by a priest or bishop; Protestants believe it comes directly from God

agnostic a person who believes that the existence of God cannot be known

anchorite a person who has retired to a solitary place for a life of religious seclusion; **anchoress** a female anchorite

Anglican church the official Church of England created between 1530 and 1600, as a result of King Henry's VIII's separation from the Roman Catholic church

animist someone who believes that natural objects, natural phenomena, and the universe itself possess souls

antinomianism the heretical belief that ministers and the established church are unnecessary

ascetic a person who practices self-denial for religious reasons

atheist a person who denies or disbelieves the existence of a supreme being

Buddhism the religion founded by Siddhartha Gautama, in India in 6th century B.C.

canonize to officially make someone a saint

Celtic Christianity the Christianity that thrived in Ireland and western England and Scotland from the time of St. Patrick to the era of the Viking raids

Church of Latter-Day Saints of Jesus Christ the church movement founded by Joseph Smith during the 19th century; also called Mormonism

cloister a place of religious seclusion

Confucianism the social code developed by Confucius in China during the sixth century B.C; it remained the most important set of Chinese beliefs until the Communists took control of China in 1949

dervish a member of any various Muslim ascetic orders, some of which practice ecstatic dancing and whirling or chanting and shouting

dogma doctrine that according to the Roman Catholic church cannot be debated or challenged (also see **infallibility**)

excommunicated to be cut off or deprived of membership in the Catholic church, and especially the ability to receive the sacraments

existentialism a 20th century philosophical movement that stresses a person's position as a self-determining individual responsible for his or her own choices

gnosticism the beliefs of second century religious sects that claimed to have a secret knowledge or revelation of God

hermit someone who lives apart from the world in order to concentrate on his or her spiritual state; the habitation of a hermit is called a *hermitage*

Hindu a follower of Hinduism, the original religion of the Indian subcontinent which has evolved slowly over more than a thousand years

icon an image that is meant to represent God

indulgences the reduction, granted by God through the Catholic church, of the time that forgiven sinners would spend in Purgatory

infallibility Roman Catholic doctrine which holds that the pope is immune from fallacy or error when he speaks on religious matters

karma in Eastern religions, such as Hinduism, Buddhism, and Jainism, the law which governs the effects of deeds both in this life and within subsequent lives

lama a Tibetan monk of high rank

monasticism a form of Christian living in which those individuals who seek God through a life of celibacy, asceticism, and prayer live in seclusion either as hermits or in religious communities called *monasteries*

monotheist someone who believes in only one God

mystic a person who comes to a deeper faith in God through an inner experience, often enhanced by meditation and prayer

novitiate the quarters occupied by a religious *novice*, a person admitted into a religious order or congregation for a period of probation before taking vows

GLOSSARY

oratories places of prayer

ordained to be invested with holy orders

pagan a person who is not a Christian, Jew, or Muslim; in ancient Rome and Greece, a person who believed in many gods (see also polytheist); an irreligious person

pantheistic someone who follows *pantheism*, the religious belief or philosophy that identifies God with the universe

papal bull a formal and important official document issued by the pope

papal interdiction a punishment issued by the pope in which the faithful are forbidden certain sacraments and prohibited from participating in certain sacred acts

papal legate someone designated by the pope as his representative

pilgrim a person who goes on a journey (pilgrimage) to enhance his or her spiritual understanding

polytheist a person who believes that there is a set of Gods

predestination the belief that people are chosen by God for eternal salvation; some controversial forms of belief hold that while some people are chosen for salvation, the rest of humanity is condemned to damnation

prior an officer in a monastic order or a religious house; a woman holding such a position is called a *prioress*

Protestant a Western Christian not an adherent of a Catholic, Anglican or Eastern church; a member of any number of religious groups that resulted from the movement begun by Martin Luther in 1517. Today there are dozens of Protestant faiths, including Methodist, Episcopalian, Congregational, Baptist, Mennonite, and Lutheran.

Puritan a Protestant movement that began during the 16th century within the Church of England whose members demanded a simpler doctrine and worship and greater strictness in religious discipline; the movement later took root in New England

rationalism the principle or habit of accepting reason as the supreme authority in matters of opinion, belief, or conduct

reincarnation the belief that the soul, upon death of the body, comes back to earth in another body or form

religious of or pertaining to religion; a member of a religious order, such as a monk or nun

sacrament one of the central Christian religious ceremonies, such as baptism and communion; seven sacraments are recognized by the Catholic and Orthodox churches

scriptures (also called Holy Scriptures) the sacred writings of the Old or New Testaments of the Bible, or both taken together; any writing or book of a scared or religious nature, such as the Koran for people of the Muslim faith

synod an assembly of members of the clergy or other church delegates that discusses and decides upon church affairs

Talmud the ancient code of Jewish law and tradition as collected, edited, and revised by the early rabbis

theocracy a system of government in which God or a deity is recognized as the supreme ruler, and in which priests or ministers rule by claiming a divine commission

Torah (Judaism) the teaching or law, handed down in both written and oral form to Moses on Sinai; identified in written form with the first five books of the Hebrew Bible (Old Testament)

transubstantiation the Roman Catholic belief that the bread and wine offered at the Eucharist—Holy Communion—actually become the body and blood of Jesus Christ, not just symbols of them

zazen a form of sitting meditation that became the core of Buddhism in Japan

Index

Index

Index